HOW TO PRONOUNCE IT

HOW TO PRONOUNCE IT

ALAN S. C. ROSS

Professor of Linguistics in the University of Birmingham (England)

HAMISH HAMILTON

LONDON

*First Published in Great Britain
by Hamish Hamilton Ltd 1970
90 Great Russell Street London W.C.1*

SBN 241 01967 2

PRINTED IN GREAT BRITAIN BY
WESTERN PRINTING SERVICES LTD., BRISTOL

FOREWORD

THE main part of this book consists of a list of certain words and names with their pronunciations; in many cases I give a right pronunciation and a wrong one. Many of these words and names are ones about whose pronunciation people are worried; some of them are considered difficult to pronounce. The reasons for the worry are, in the main, either social or educational, or both. Englishmen feel very strongly about the pronunciation of words and names, and, indeed, some of them are often angry about it. What I have written will thus provoke criticisms; either because of pronunciations which I advocate, or allow, or of which I disapprove; or because of omissions. All such criticisms will be welcome, and I hope that readers will send them in to me so that I may consider them for use in future possible editions. For advice on various points I am very grateful to: Miss Dorothy Atkinson, Commander G. Borrett *R.N.*, Mr. J. H. Eaton, Mr. Charles Gore, Mr. Hamish Hamilton, Professor V. Kiparsky, Mrs. Larminie, Dr. E. H. Linfoot, Professor J. Manson, Mr. Colin Prichard, Dr. Peter Ricketts, Dr. W. van der Will, Professor A. Vos, and—especially—to my wife; further to various clergy-men, croquet-players, school-masters and -mistresses, and bearers of individual surnames, unfortunately too numerous to mention specifically.

ALAN S. C. ROSS

Department of Linguistics,
P.O. Box 363, The University, Birmingham 15, England

v

INTRODUCTION

CLEARLY, any book on Pronunciation must begin with an account of how Pronunciation will be described in that book. The description of Pronunciation—that is, the description of something spoken by means of something written—is well-known to afford a difficult problem. The learned solution to this problem is—the Phonetic Alphabet. This Alphabet—or, rather, system of signs—has been devised during the last hundred years precisely in order that it may accurately describe in writing the spoken form of any language. It will thus deal adequately with things as far apart as the clicks of Zulu or the two vowel-sounds which make English so hard for the foreigner to pronounce, namely the sound of *u* in *but*, and the sound of *a* in *china*.

Naturally, the Phonetic Alphabet is of some complexity. To learn it, and to learn how to use it, is a task more difficult than that of learning, and learning how to use, either the Greek or the Russian alphabet. Neither of the last two tasks is in fact particularly arduous, but I have felt that to use the Phonetic Alphabet would be a considerable worry to many readers of a book which is, essentially, non-learned.

The normal spoken English of England is made up of combinations of about forty-four basic speech-sounds or 'phonemes', as they are technically called.[1]

For a perfect alphabet it is obvious that each spoken phoneme must be represented by one and only one letter, and each letter

---

[1] 'About' may seem most unscientific. But the number of phonemes used by different speakers of English does vary. Those who pronounce *poor* the same as *paw* have one phoneme less than those who do not; while those who do not pronounce *which* the same as *witch* have one phoneme more than those who do.

1

must represent one and only one phoneme. The goodness of an alphabet may be measured by how near it is to perfection; and an alphabet that is not good may be said to be bad. The English alphabet is one of the worst in the world; the sound of *f* in *fun* is represented by the letter *f* in that word, but by the combination of letters, *gh*, in *rough*. On the other hand this same combination of letters, *gh*, can, in *ghost*, also represent the sound of *g* in *gun*, while, in *though*, the letters *gh* represent nothing at all—that is they are silent. The word *rough* has five letters, but only three phonemes. The English alphabet really is bad; after all, on the analogy of other words, we could spell the word *fish* as *ghoti*, if we used *gh* pronounced as in *rough*, *o* as in *women*, and *ti* as in *station*.

The English alphabet has not always been as bad as it is to-day. In the fourteenth century it was quite good. But, since then, there have been many changes in pronunciation—'sound-changes', that is, changes in the way in which words are pronounced. The spelling did not, however, follow the sound-changes; we still use what is essentially a fourteenth-century spelling. And the coming of Printing gradually made this spelling standard, for, naturally, a system of spelling that is standard is more convenient to Printers than one that is not. The fact that the spelling has not been altered to conform with the major sound-changes is, effectively, why the vowels of English are not 'continental'. Any European, seeing the English word *ride* for the first time, would naturally pronounce it as we do the word *read*; in the fourteenth century *ride* was approximately so pronounced, but, since then, it has gradually changed into its modern pronunciation; the spelling has, however, remained correct for a pronunciation identical with that of *read*, but clearly bizarre for the pronunciation the word actually has.

Shaw left money for the perfecting of an English alphabet and, to-day, there are reformed, perfect, English alphabets in existence. These are intended primarily for children learning to read, for it is clearly easier to learn to read by means of a good alphabet than by means of a bad one. The difficulty is, of course, that, since virtually all English is written in the standard bad alphabet, the children have, soon, to change over from the perfect alphabet they have learnt to the bad, ordinary one.

English is not the only language with a bad alphabet; that of French is not at all good: *tant, temps, t'en* and *taon* are pronounced the same, but spelt differently. On the other hand, many languages have very good alphabets. The Finnish alphabet is almost perfect; so, too, is that of Welsh—if we allow certain combinations of two letters to rank as one letter (*ll* in *Llanelly* is one phoneme, not two).

It may be noted that there is a simple, practical test for the goodness of an alphabet: How soon does the beginner become perfect in taking dictation? Those who teach foreigners English know that they do not attain perfection in this for years. But the beginner in Welsh or Finnish may be quite good at it after the very first lesson.

Since I am not going to use the Phonetic Alphabet in this book, I have devised a system of representing the pronunciation. I give the representation in square brackets [ ].

The system is the following:

a	*represents the sound of*	a *in* pat
ah	,,	ar *in* cart
aw	,,	aw *in* paw
ay	,,	ay *in* day
b	,,	b *in* bin
ch	,,	ch *in* chin
d	,,	d *in* din
dh	,,	th *in* then
e	,,	e *in* bet
ee	,,	ee *in* seen
eeə	,,	eer *in* deer
ɛi	,,	ie *in* tie
ɛə	,,	ere *in* there
f	,,	f *in* fun
g	,,	g *in* gun

3

h	*represents the sound of* h *in* hat	
i	,,	i *in* pit
j	,,	j *in* jet
k	,,	k *in* kin
l	,,	l *in* lump
m	,,	m *in* mat
n	,,	n *in* nut
ng	,,	ng *in* sing
o	,,	o *in* hot
oh	,,	o *in* go
oi	,,	oi *in* oil
oo	,,	oo *in* boot
ooə	,,	our *in* tour
ou	,,	ou *in* found
p	,,	p *in* pin
r	,,	r *in* run
s	,,	s *in* sat
sh	,,	sh *in* ship
t	,,	t *in* tin
th	,,	th *in* thin
ur	,,	ur *in* fur
ʊ	,,	u *in* pull
v	,,	v *in* vat
w	,,	w *in* win
y	,,	y *in* yacht
z	,,	z *in* zeal
zh	,,	ge *in* beige
ʌ	,,	u *in* but
ə	,,	a *in* china

Much of the above system is obvious. Thus, the meaning of the following thirty-four of the forty-four letters or letter-combinations must immediately be clear to the reader: *ah, aw, ay, b, ch, d, e, ee, f, g, h, i, j, k, l, m, n, ng, o, oh, oi, oo, ou, p, r, s, sh, t, th, ur, v, w, y, z.* Of the remaining ten, *a* (*a* in *cat*) should not be troublesome, for many English *a*'s are pronounced in this way. *dh* (*th* in *then*) and *zh* (*ge* in *beige*) are well recognised representations. It has been necessary to use two symbols from the Phonetic Alphabet: ʌ (inverted *v*) for *u* in *but* and ə (inverted *e*) for *a* in *china*; there are no other satisfactory representations for them; for instance, *uh* for the latter, often used, is not satisfactory, because, to some speakers at least, it can suggest quite a different sound. Having established ə, it is natural to use it in the two combinations *eeə* and *ooə*, for these phonemes, *eer* in *deer* and *our* in *tour*, are, in fact, compound phonemes, made up, respectively, of *ee*+ə (*ee* in *seen* and ə in *china*) and *oo*+ə (*oo* in *boot* and ə in *china*). There is, further, no satisfactory representation of *ie* in *tie*; I have therefore used εi (with Greek epsilon) for it; this does suggest the sound. Having used ε (Greek epsilon) once, there seems no reason against using it again—in εə for *ere* in *there*. There remains the sound of *u* in *pull*; since I have not used *u* by itself at all, it might have been thought that I should use it in this function; but, taken by itself, *u* suggests *u* in *but* not *pull*. I have therefore used ʊ (Greek ypsilon) which, at least, looks like *u*.

As I have already said, spoken English consists of various combinations of its phonemes. The phonemes are thus the primary ingredients—the atoms—of the language. But besides them, there are two other ingredients, *Accentuation* and *Intonation*.

Combinations of phonemes form *Syllables*. Thus the word *but* [bʌt] is one syllable, whereas the word *butter* [bʌt-ə] has two syllables. I separate the syllables by hyphens. In English the *Accent* (or, *Stress*) can fall on any syllable of a word. Thus *revel* has two syllables, and the accent falls on the first; *revile* also has two syllables, and the accent falls on the second. In this book, I indicate the accent by underlining the vowel-phoneme of the accented syllable in the printed representation of the pronunciation; thus *revel* [rᴇv-əl] and *revile* [rə-vᴇil]. English accentuation is a little more complicated than as set out above. In long words, there is usually, in addition to the main accent, a secondary accent. Thus *suitability* has five syllables; the main accent is on the

5

third syllable, but there is a secondary accent on the first. To indicate the secondary accent in this book would be impracticable; I therefore omit it, and, thus, I should merely give the pronunciation of *suitability* as [syoo-tə-bil-i-ti], with no mark on the *oo*. My failure to mark the secondary accent will, however, cause but little trouble to the reader. In almost all words, once the main accent is known, the secondary accent falls into place almost automatically.

Not many pairs of English words are distinguished solely by their accent. However, the verb *present* has the accent on the second syllable, [prəz-ent], whereas the corresponding noun, *present*, has the accent on the first, [prez-ənt]. This verb and noun do therefore form such a pair.

Another feature of English accentuation should be mentioned here, namely that usually called *Level Stress*. The phonemes of the two sentences *It's a blackbird* and *It's a black bird* are, of course, identical, though the two are differently printed. But there is a difference both in meaning and pronunciation between them. The first sentence means 'It's a special kind of bird, for instance, it's not a thrush', while the second refers to the colour of the bird—it is not, for instance, a yellow bird. And, in the first sentence, *blackbird* has only one main accent—on *black*, while, in the second, *black bird* has two main accents, one on *black*, the other on *bird*; the stress of *black bird* is thus said to be *level*, whereas that of *blackbird* is not. Thus:

It's a blackbird [its ə blakburd]
It's a black bird [its ə blak burd].

Intonation is the musical rise and fall of the speaker's voice along the sentence. Its nature can be made clear by means of an example. The word *Really!*—which is a sentence consisting of just one word—when said by a second speaker in answer to a statement by a first speaker, is normally pronounced [reeə-li],[1] but there is a number of different ways in which the second speaker can utter the word; he may, for instance, thereby express

[1] Here I omit from the discussion other pronunciations, such as [ree-li], to rhyme with *mealie*, for which see p. 148.

6

either boredom at or interest in the first speaker's remark. *Yes* and *No* can also be uttered with many different intonations.[1]

Intonation is a most important linguistic feature. It can affect whole languages. Thus the statement 'He has a strong Welsh accent' really means, not so much that the person referred to uses non-English pronunciation, but, rather, that he speaks English with the intonation used in speaking Welsh. Since a child primarily learns to speak from its parents, this kind of intonation can persist from generation to generation so that there are to-day Welsh people who speak with a Welsh accent, despite the fact that even their grandparents did not speak Welsh. Intonation is one of the things that people most notice. Visitors to Jamaica frequently say that Jamaicans speak with a Welsh accent. It is the fact that, to normal English ears, Jamaican English does sound rather like Welsh English. The explanation is quite straightforward. Just as Welsh English is English spoken with the intonation of Welsh, so Jamaican English is English spoken with the intonation of the assortment of African languages—mostly West African languages—spoken by the slaves. By chance, the two resulting intonations are similar. The fact that no African language has been spoken in Jamaica for generations does not affect the issue; African intonation persists among non-African-speaking Jamaicans just as Welsh intonation persists among non-Welsh-speaking Welshmen.

In the languages of Europe there are extremely few pairs of words which are distinguished solely by their intonation[2]—

[1] But also with different pronunciations. Thus, on Television, *yes* pronounced [yays], to rhyme with *pace*, has been used—notably by the late Mr. Freddie Frinton—to indicate a lower-class speaker's facetious aping of upper-class speech. And, in my time at Oxford, there was that Wadham don who almost invariably pronounced *yes* identically with *arse*. [yurs], to rhyme with *purse*, is also known. Forms without the final consonant, such as [ye] and [yɛə], are often used; in part, they may be apings of American— the American form is often written *yeah*—as the altered forms [yep], to rhyme with *pep*, and [yʌp], to rhyme with *pup*, certainly are.

[2] There is such a pair in Norwegian. The words *bønner* and *bønder* consist of exactly the same phonemes in the same order—*nn* and *nd* are both pronounced the same as single [n] (*n* in *nut*). The first word means 'beans',

in English there are none. In some geographical groups of languages, however, extremely many pairs of words are distinguished only by their intonation. The best-known example of this kind of 'tonal' language is Chinese; there are several other tonal languages in the Far East, also many in West Africa and Central America.

In the case of Chinese and other tonal languages it is thus essential that the intonation be indicated in the representation of the pronunciation. Such indication requires the addition of a complex system of signs to the Phonetic Alphabet. Often a musical notation is used. The intonation of spoken English can be shown in the same way. I do not attempt any indication of the intonation in this book. Nor is it necessary, for the subject of the book is essentially the pronunciation and mispronunciation of individual words, a subject into which intonation hardly enters.

I am here only concerned with the spoken English of the British Isles. Forms of English spoken outside this area, for instance in regions colonised by the English, be they large (such as the U.S.A.), or small (such as Pitcairn Island), do not come within my terms of reference. Both American English and Pitcairn English are very different from English English.

The spoken English of the British Isles is of many different kinds, though the written language is the same throughout the country. The kind varies—according to the place the speaker lives in, according to his social class, and according to the amount of education he has received. The main dividing line is between the Regional Dialects on the one hand and the Standard Englishes on the other. The Regional Dialects differ from the Standards not only in pronunciation and grammar but also in vocabulary—especially in that part of it that relates to rural things. In England the Regional Dialects, though spoken to-day only by those members of the lowest classes who are poorly educated, still survive, but in a much weaker form than they had

the second 'farmers'. The intonation of the two words is different, and this keeps them apart.

8

seventy years ago when Professor Joseph Wright compiled his great *English Dialect Dictionary*. Dialect is much more flourishing in some parts of the country than in others. Thus Scotch dialect thrives whereas Sussex dialect hardly exists—here the influence of London has been too great.

The Standard Englishes are regional: there is, for example, a London Standard, a Leeds Standard, an Irish Standard and a Scotch Standard. Curiously, some very large places have no Standard; Birmingham has absolutely none. The division between the dialects and the Regional Standards is not hard-and-fast; the latter have been much influenced by the former.

There is one form of Standard English that is paramount and not associated with any particular region. This has been called 'Received Standard English' but I have preferred to call it 'U-English'. It is in fact the English of the class I have called 'U'. I originally used the term 'U' as an abbreviation for *Upper Class*, and it is this class which, almost without exception, uses U-English. Many of the non-U—by which term I mean persons who are not U—aspire to speak U-English; if they know that they can never speak it themselves, they hope that at least their children, or even their grandchildren will. Non-U English is full of 'shibboleths';[1] and U-English is, in some sort, merely the avoiding of non-U features.

[1] I use this word advisedly. Essentially, it means 'a linguistic peculiarity which denotes a person's origin' and its use derives from the following story in the twelfth chapter of the Book of Judges: 'Then Jephthah gathered together all the men of Gilead, and fought with Ephraim ... And the Gileadites took the passages of Jordan before the Ephraimites: and it was so, that when those Ephraimites which were escaped said, Let me go over; that the men of Gilead said unto him, Art thou an Ephraimite? If he said, Nay; Then said they unto him, Say now Shibboleth: and he said Sibboleth; for he could not frame to pronounce it right. Then they took him, and slew him at the passages of Jordan: and there fell at that time of the Ephraimites forty and two thousand.' There were dialects in Hebrew—just as there are in English—and the Ephraimites used [s] in place of normal Hebrew [sh]. *Shibboleth* may be either the Hebrew word meaning 'ear of grain' or that meaning 'stream'. There was of course nothing special about the word *shibboleth*; presumably any other Hebrew word beginning with [sh] would have done as well. In the last War, members of the Dutch Resistance picked

This book is essentially a book on Language, not one on Class. I shall therefore not attempt here the very difficult task of defining the U class. I may, however, give some indication of its nature by saying that the main task of Public School education is to keep its U-boys U and turn its non-U boys into U-boys. In this task, the Public Schools still have a great measure of success. This is well-recognised, and non-U fathers crowd the waiting-lists with the names of children who may one day pass as, and may even be, quite U. To-day the Universities are not at all in the same case as the Public Schools. Oxford and Cambridge are no longer predominantly U. (In concluding this paragraph I may refer the reader, first, to the book *Noblesse Oblige*, edited by Nancy Mitford, in which my essay 'U and non-U' appeared. Secondly to the book *What are U?*, which I have just edited.)

The categories 'U' and 'Educated' do not by any means coincide. Stories setting forth the erudition and wide interests of peasants abound. 'Ah,' said the Shetlander who was deeply interested in the Russo–Japanese War, 'so you're a Professor. You're the first person I've met who'll be able to tell me the size of the harbour at Vladivostok.' Or, again, I was interested in an ancient monument, in a remote part of Wales, called *Crugiau Ladies*. *Crugiau* means 'rocks', but *Ladies* is not clear; it can hardly be *Wladys* (the mutated form of the Welsh girl's name *Gwladys*—spelt *Gladys* in English), nor can it be the English word *ladies*. 'Well,' said the shepherd, 'I shouldn't be surprised if the name of the Emperor Claudius may not lie concealed there.' Then there was the Cuban porter at the railway station at Santiago de Oriente. I was carrying a copy of Camões' Lusíadas. '¡Oh! La ruta India', said the porter. Nor have I forgotten the Birmingham policeman whose hobby was Calculus. There are stories the other way round too. 'That's an

out Nazi spies in their midst by the latters' inability to pronounce correctly the name of the Dutch town, *Ijmuiden*—it is indeed very difficult for the non-Dutch; perhaps the best that an Englishman can do is [ɛi-mɐid-ə], first syllable the same as *eye*, last two to rhyme with *rider*.

10

ambiguous remark,' I said to a U-girl many years ago. '*Ambiguous*,' she replied, 'a good word, I must remember it.' One must not be too hard on the U however. After all, many intellectuals do not know the difference between *scatological* and *eschatalogical*.

The U are hurt if you suggest that they are uneducated. They feel that they must be educated because they have been to a 'good school'. Alas, this is an illusion. In brief it can be said that there is no discernible difference in education between U and non-U.

I am now able to discuss the terms of reference of this book. It is primarily concerned with the pronunciations of individual words and names, and, in it, my aim is, in the main, to distinguish between U or educated pronunciation on the one hand, and non-U or uneducated pronunciation on the other. Thus *Derby* is pronounced [da̲h̲-bi], first syllable to rhyme with *car*,[1] by the U, but [du̲r-bi], first syllable to rhyme with *cur*, by the non-U. The educated pronounce *amicable* with the accent on the first syllable, [a̲m-ik-ə-bəl], the uneducated with the accent on the second, [am-i̲k-ə-bəl]. I therefore include both these in my *List of Words and Names*, entering the former as '. . . [da̲h̲-bi] . . . NOT [du̲r-bi]', and the latter as '. . . [a̲m-ik-ə-bəl] . . . NOT [am-i̲k-ə-bəl]'. From this form of entry it will be seen, first, that I do not distinguish between 'non-U' and 'uneducated'—indeed it would be very difficult to do so; and, secondly, that the first pronunciation given is the U or educated one, while the second, often preceded by the word NOT, is the non-U or uneducated one. Since I consider the U or educated pronunciation to be 'better' or 'more correct' than the non-U or uneducated one, I

---

[1] As a help to the reader I try to implement my phonetic description of the pronunciation by means of rhymes whenever this is possible. Thus I indicate the correct pronunciation of *aspect* by saying that its first syllable rhymes with *gas*, not *farce*. In some cases there are no rhymes; thus it is not possible to distinguish between the U and non-U pronunciations of *solve*— that is [solv] and [sohlv] respectively—by means of rhymes. Often I use the expression 'the same as' instead of giving a rhyme; for example 'BACUP, Lancashire . . . first syllable the same as *bake*. NOT . . . the same as *back*.'

11

frequently use the terms *good, better, correct,* etc., with this implication. With *possible* or *admissible,* the words 'for U-speakers' are to be understood. By a *mispronunciation,* I mean one made by the non-U or uneducated. I may note here that the mispronunciations are almost all ones actually heard by me; a small residue are ones where the spelling could very easily lead to a mispronunciation. *Normal* means that a pronunciation is used by most people, of whatever class or education. In some cases I give only one pronunciation; this is the U or educated pronunciation and implies that I know no other. I include these cases because, in them, the spelling may easily lead the uninitiated astray into a mispronunciation. In very many other cases, there really are two equally admissible pronunciations; thus *fanatic* can properly be pronounced either with the accent on the first syllable [fan-ə-tik]; or with the accent on the second [fən-a-tik].[1]

My *List of Words and Names* must, of its nature, include entries of the most varied character. The names are those of persons and of geographical entities (such as towns).

Foreign geographical names deserve a slight comment here. They are of two kinds. (A) Many have anglicised forms and are thus truly part of the English language; these forms do not correspond very closely with the modern forms in the languages from which they come. (B) Other names do not have anglicised forms and are thus not truly part of the English language. They are pronounced in a manner which the English speaker thinks an approximation to the true foreign pronunciation. Unless the speaker knows the foreign language concerned, this pronunciation must of course always be slightly wrong, because the phonemes of two languages are not the same. And, if a speaker who does know the foreign language pronounces the name correctly,

---

[1] It is this first pronunciation which has given rise to the abbreviation *fan.* This was used in America for a keen supporter of a sport, particularly baseball; hence it came to have a more general meaning, namely an enthusiast for a thing or a person. It is in this last sense that it is used to-day in England also—the fans of a film-star or a pop-singer.

he will certainly be thought to be affected and showing-off. Thus *Tours* belongs to Type B—it is pronounced by most English speakers in a way somewhat resembling the way it is pronounced in French; so, too, is *Rouen*; it is a long time since this had an anglicised, Type A pronunciation—the Anglo-Saxons, however, called it *Rothem*. The anglicised pronunciations of Type A always bear some relation to their foreign originals, even if this is not a very close one. In English we have nothing so bizarre and different from the original as Hungarian *Bécs* meaning 'Vienna', Welsh *Rhydychen* meaning 'Oxford' or Czech *Kodaň* meaning 'Copenhagen'. *Paris* [pạ-ris], to rhyme with *Harris*, is a good example of an anglicised pronunciation of Type A. Its Type B pronunciation [pa-rẹẹ] is only used as an Edwardian joke—*gay Paree*. To pronounce *Amsterdam*, *Lisbon*, *Llanelly* and *Madrid* in the—very un-English—way in which they are pronounced by the relevant foreigners would be unbearably pedantic.

My *List of Words and Names* thus covers the minutiæ of the differences in pronunciation between U and non-U, educated and uneducated. I cannot hope that it is exhaustive, and I have intentionally omitted many examples. Thus I do not include the wine-name *Chablis*, for, in English, this merely has a French pronunciation without final S.

There are extremely many minutiæ in the pronunciation-differences discussed in this book. There is also another, and perhaps more fundamental way in which pronunciation and mispronunciation differ. This is when a pronunciation-difference concerns not a single, individual word, but, rather, every occurrence of a particular phoneme. Thus [ou], the sound of *ou* in *found*, is pronounced by many non-U speakers in a manner different from that in which it is pronounced by all U-speakers. And, for these non-U speakers, this is true of every occurrence of the phoneme [ou]—thus in *mouse*, *round*, *howl* also.

I attempt next an enumeration of some of these major differences in the phonemes. Again, I cannot hope that my enumeration is exhaustive. And the cognoscenti will appreciate how very much I am here handicapped by my resolution (p. 1) not to use the Phonetic Alphabet.

Essentially, English has only single consonants, not double ones. In this it is unlike many languages. Both Finnish and Italian have the last. In Finnish *kukka* meaning 'flower' the *k* is articulated twice, whereas, in the genitive singular of this word, *kukan* 'of a flower', it is only articulated once. And in Italian *fratello* meaning 'brother', *l* is sounded for a longer period of time than it is in *nobile* meaning 'noble'. Finnish has a double L too; *kyllä* meaning 'certainly' (with long L), which is different from *kylä* meaning 'village' (with short L).[1] English only has double consonants in compound words such as *book-case* [bʊk-kays] and *pen-knife* [pɛn-nɛif], the two syllables being equally stressed (see p. 6) and, in these cases, some old U-speakers simplify the double consonant and say [bʊk-ays], [pɛn-ɛif], with only one accent.

The best-known consonantal mispronunciation is the 'dropping of H'. It is the case that initial [h] (*h* in *hat*) is not pronounced—is completely silent—for many speakers, but not for U or educated ones. This loss of [h] is found in many dialects, but not in all (for instance, not in those of Scotland). For a nouveau riche to 'drop his aitches' has long been a standard English joke—see Punch, nineteenth century, *passim*. This loss of H leads to misplacing it; those who have lost it put it on in the wrong places when trying to improve their English and say, for instance, *hall* instead of *all*. There is another pronunciation-feature connected with H, of quite a different kind. The indefinite article exists in two forms, *a* and *an*, the former being used before a consonant (*a dog*), the latter before a vowel (*an engine*). In words in which initial H is silent, the latter form is naturally

---

[1] Italian and Finnish are, by other Europeans, considered very beautiful languages. Furthermore to, English ears, Italian and Finnish sound alike; if you know a little Italian but no Finnish, Finns—at least at a distance—sound as if they were talking Italian. No one knows what makes a language sound beautiful. It may be that the reason why Italian and Finnish sound beautiful and that they sound alike to the English is nothing more than their possession of a double L, a very trivial matter.

used (*an hour*).[1] But some speakers use *an* before H even when it is sounded—provided the word is not accented on the first syllable. Thus, while, like most other people, they say *a history* [his-tri], these speakers say *an historic event* [his-to̞-rik] instead of the more usual *a historic event*. The usage is pedantic and—possibly—rather female.

The distinction in pronunciation between *wh* and *w* is probably a more important consonantal feature. Many speakers pronounce *wh* in *which* differently from *w* in *witch*. Of these a few merely pronounce [h] in front of the [w]—thus *which* as [hwich]. But, for most such speakers, *wh* is not two sounds [hw], but one, and the way in which it is made can be explained very simply. There is only one difference between the sounds [s] (*s* in *sat*) and [z] (*z* in *zeal*), that is, that, in the making of [z], the glottis vibrates, whereas in the making of [s] it does not. Vibration of the glottis can be felt by putting a finger on the Adam's apple. Now, to make the sound of *wh*, make [w] (*w* in *win*), but do not let the glottis vibrate while doing so. To-day, WH seems to be predominately female, and its distribution has nothing to do with U and non-U, or with education. Most male speakers (except the Irish) do not possess it and pronounce *which* the same as *witch*, that is, both with [w] (*w* in *win*).

Above I have given [ng] as *ng* in *sing*, by which I mean *sing* as pronounced by the U. For them, written *ng* represents one single sound.[2] But there is a non-U pronunciation, widespread in the Midlands, in which written *ng* does not represent one sound, but two; these speakers pronounce *sing* as [singg] and *singer* as [sing-gə]. 'Dropping the G' of [ng]—a bad phonetic description

[1] Just as we have *a* and *an*, so we used to have *my* and *mine*. The latter occasionally survives as an archaism, as in *mine eyes*. H used to be silent in the word *host* and the N survives in *mine host* beside *my host*.

[2] That it really is one single sound can be seen by comparing it with [g]. The sound [ng] is, in fact [g], with the breath expelled via the nasal passages. So that, if you have a cold and thus cannot use these, you will produce [ng] as [g] and say [sig], to rhyme with *big*, instead of [sing]. [d] and the nasal [n] form a comparable pair to [g] and [ng]; if you have a cold you will pronounce *nice* identically with *dice*.

meaning to pronounce [n] instead of [ng]—as in *Huntin'*, *shootin'* and *fishin'*, is well known. It certainly survived into the 'twenties but, even then, sounded silly and affected unless used by the very old U. Now it exists only as a joke, usually made by the non-U against the U.

In Irish Standard certain consonants are heavily aspirated. In making [b] (*b* in *bin*), there is an expulsion of breath after the closure of the lips. In Ireland more breath is expelled than in England; this pronunciation is often indicated by spellings such as *bhoy* for *boy*. [p] and [t] are similarly over-aspirated, as in *pin*, *tin*.[1] I may note here that many Irish speakers cannot pronounce [th] (*th* in *thin*) and substitute [t] (*t* in *tin*) for it: *trobbing* for *throbbing*. Another Irishism concerns [i] (*i* in *pit*) and [e] (*e* in *bet*) when these are unaccented. They are pronounced [ə] (*a* in *china*) or even [ʌ] (*u* in *but*); thus *it* in *I did it* is [ət] or [ʌt]; *'em* in *That won't help 'em* (i.e. *help them*) is [əm] or [ʌm].

There is considerable variation in the pronunciation of R. The best-known variant is the Scotch R which is very distinctive but cannot be described without giving the phonetic details. It is to this R that the expression 'rolling one's R's' applies. This is indeed a fair description. R used to be called 'the dog's letter' because its sound was considered to resemble the snarling of a dog. Children who had French governesses used a French *r* in all English words and many retain this feature throughout life. Such one-time children are, to-day, mostly old U people, statistically more female than male. The insertion of R between vowels —*I sawr it* for *I saw it*—is much used by non-U speakers. Also by children, U and non-U. It is a well-known fault in bad singers—*I'm off to Philadelphia rin the morning* as the Victorian song has it.

The glottal stop is known to most people from Glaswegian pronunciations such as *wa'er* for *water*. It is used by many speakers, particularly the London non-U, instead of T in many words, for instance [kǫ'-ən] cotton, [ə lǫ' ov] *a lot of*.

Only two short English vowels require comment. (1) [a] (*a* in

---

[1] In the well-known Irish word *Throubles*, the TH represents the over-aspiration of the [t] of *troubles*.

16

pat). To pronounce *pat* as *pet*—and every [a] as [e]—is regarded as the sign of a non-U 'effeminate' young man—to the describers 'effeminate' probably often means 'homosexual'; for some peculiar reason modern actresses tend to use an un-English vowel for [a] (*a* in *pat*), namely the sound of *a* in German *hat* (which means 'has'). The result is not dissimilar to the Leeds pronunciation of [a]—often referred to, for no obvious reason, as 'flat'.[1] (2) ʌ (*u* in *but*). In many dialects of the North of England —and in the corresponding Standards (e.g. that of Leeds)—this vowel is pronounced [u] in many words; so that *dull* is pronounced to rhyme with the normal pronunciation of *bull*. Those who try to improve their English by altering this state of affairs to that obtaining in normal English, often get things wrong and substitute [ʌ] for a correct [u]; they thus pronounce *butcher* as [bʌch-ə], first syllable to rhyme with the normal pronunciation of *such*. The phenomenon is parallel to that of 'misplaced H' (see above).

English is remarkably deficient in long vowels; there are only three: [ah] (*ar* in *cart*), [aw] (*aw* in *paw*), and [ur] (*ur* in *fur*). The other English sounds usually thought of as long vowels are, in fact, diphthongs, though no Englishman untrained in Phonetics does—or can—appreciate this fact. A *diphthong* is a combination of two vowels; that in *oil* is a very clear example; the two vowels which are combined in it are [o] (*o* in *hot*) and [i] (*i* in *pit*). Any native English-speaker can easily satisfy himself that this really is so by 'trying it out'. A *triphthong* is a combination of three vowels.

[ɛi] (*ie* in *tie*) and [ou] (*ou* in *found*) are indeed usually thought of as diphthongs. The following four diphthongs are, however, always thought of, not as diphthongs, but as long vowels:

[ay] (*ay* in *day*) = [e] (*e* in *bet*)+[i] (*i* in *pit*);
[ee] (*ee* in *seen*) = [i] (*i* in *pit*)+another [i] (*i* in *pit*);

[1] The sound of German *a* in *hat* is almost identical with English [ʌ] (*u* in *but*). This sound [ʌ] is felt to be very difficult by foreigners learning English; in their schools, they are, apparently, taught to pronounce English *hut* the same as English *hot*. If only the Germans could learn to say their *hat* for our *hut*!

17

[oh] (*o* in *go*) = the sound formed by making [o] (*o* in *hot*) with more than the usual closure of the lips+[ʊ] (*u* in *pull*);

[oo] (*oo* in *boot*) = [ʊ] (*u* in *pull*)+another [ʊ] (*u* in *pull*).

The difference between the diphthongs last mentioned and true long vowels is well seen from the statement 'German *tee* (which means "tea") is not pronounced the same as [the River] *Tay* in English'—German *ee* is a true long vowel.

Of the six diphthongs mentioned in the last paragraph, three occasion mispronunciations.

For U-speakers [ɛi] (*ie* in *tie*) consists of either [ə] (*a* in *china*) or *a* of German *hat*+[i] (*i* in *pit*). There is a non-U pronunciation known as 'refined'—in which the first element of this diphthong is either [a] (*a* in *cat*) or [e] (*e* in *bet*). So in this pronunciation, *ride* almost rhymes with *raid*, and the second syllable of *refined* almost rhymes with *brained*. In writing, the type of pronunciation is thus often indicated by the spelling *refained*.

For the diphthong [oh] (*o* in *go*), described above, some non-U speakers have a triphthong made by prefixing [a] (*a* in *cat*) to the normal U diphthong.

For U-speakers [ou] (*ou* in *found*) is parallel to [ɛi] (*ie* in *tie*); it consists of either [ə] (*a* in *china*) or *a* of German *hat*+[ʊ] (*u* in *pull*). Some non-U speakers have here a parallel to the 'refained' pronunciation of [ɛi]; the first element of their diphthong is [a] (*a* in *cat*). This pronunciation is felt to be particularly ugly by U-speakers, and attempts are often made to indicate it in the spelling (*haows* for *house*).

In my list of English phonemes (pp. 3–4), I have given [ooə], the sound of *our* in *tour*. It is the case that many people, U and non-U alike, do have this sound in a number of words (and, particularly, in *tour*). But many U-speakers substitute [aw] (*aw* in *paw*) for it in several words of the group, and, for instance, pronounce *poor* the same as *paw*, and *moor* the same as *more*. The triphthong in words such as *wire* tends, too, to be eliminated by some U-speakers. This triphthong is the diphthong [ɛi] (*ie* in *tie*) +[ə] (*a* in *china*); thus *wire* is [wɛiə]. But some U-speakers say [wah], to rhyme with *car*.

18

A non-U pronunciation of the diphthong [ɛə] (*ere* in *there*) has recently come to the fore; this is the Manchester–Liverpool long vowel [ur] (*ur* in *fur*) for this diphthong—that is, *hair* is pronounced the same as *her*. This pronunciation is used in *Coronation Street* on Television and by the famous—and various—pop-singers from Liverpool.

I may mention here another pronunciation used by pop-singers. *New* is normally pronounced [nyoo], to rhyme with *you*. In American it is, however, pronounced [noo], to rhyme with *do*. There are several similar words with [yoo] (e.g. *dew*). English pop-singers pronounce these in the American way, doubtless because they do not wish to offend possible American buyers of their records. (It is no doubt for the same reason that they say *carrousel* when they mean *round-about*. Though this can hardly be the reason why the disc-jockeys on the Wireless say *ten minutes before nine* or *ten minutes after nine* instead of the normal English *ten to nine* and *ten past nine*.)

Finally I may mention [ə] (*a* in *china*). With some speakers this is almost [ah] (*ar* in *cart*); thus [chɛin-ah]. This pronunciation is thought of either as pertaining to Anglo-Indian colonels —these are now old—(*When I was in Poona*, with *Poona* as [poo-nah], not the normal [poo-nə], to rhyme with *sooner*). Or as 'affected'. The undergraduate, reading English at Oxford, had swotted up on his Chaucer, but was weak on Shakespeare. 'I thought this paper was [chaw-sah]' he said as he entered the Examination Schools. 'No, unfortunately, it's [shayks-pyah]' was the reply. The pronunciation of [ə] as [ah] also occurs when this sound is the second element of the diphthong [eeə]. This form of pronunciation can convert the diphthong into something approaching [yah]: [mɛi deeah] or [mɛi dyah] *My dear!* This is a predominantly female or homosexual feature.

I may conclude this *Introduction* by considering—very briefly —how far the difference between U and non-U, between educated and uneducated, is reflected in the pronunciation of languages other than English.

The second difference can be dismissed forthwith by saying

that all civilised languages recognise an uneducated pronunciation of, or conception of, certain of their words—rare, learned,
or merely rather long. Such matters are the material of innumer-
able jokes, often directed against the nouveaux riches. In Danish
the definite article is something added at the end of a word, not
put before it, as in French or English. So, while *hus* means
'house', *huset* means 'the house'. The simple Danish peasant,
hearing the word *Tibet* for the first time, has been known to
regard *-et* here as his definite article, and thus call the country
Tib. Since medical words are learned words often heard by very
uneducated people, they are especially likely to give rise to jokes
of this kind. Thus, German peasants have been known to con-
fuse *bazillen* (which means 'bacilli') with *pastillen* (which means
'pastilles'). There are comparable English medical jokes, but
these usually concern the meanings of words—such as 'I've got
such a terrible gastric stomach, doctor'—*gastric* simply means
'pertaining to the stomach'. Or, 'He's got blood-pressure'—the
blood is always at *some* pressure, it is whether this is high or low
that is medically interesting. The silliness of this last is paralleled
in the expression *atom-free zone*, used in the journalese of inter-
national affairs, to mean an area without nuclear weapons—the
earth and everything on it is made up of atoms.

The U/non-U differences of other languages are harder to
extract.

In France, differences of this kind hardly exist. It is not to be
thought, for instance, that to say *chais pas* for *je ne sais pas*
implies anything at all; it is a colloquialism that could be used
by anyone. Nor does any stigma attach to a regional accent. A
Frenchman, of any class, who possesses one, is usually rather
proud of it. But perhaps the pronunciation of foreign words is
relevant here. The English word *club* has been borrowed into
French; in *club de jeunesse*, which means 'youth-club', *club* is
pronounced as if it were a French word—that is with the French
vowel—but it would be considered rather uneducated to pronounce it in this way in *le Jockey Club*; here, most Frenchmen
make an attempt at the English pronunciation, difficult as they

find it. And, if you are a Frenchman, it is better to attempt the English pronunciation of *yacht* than to pronounce it the same as you do the animal-name *yak*.

In Italian there is a U/non-U situation and it is one of some complexity. It has been well discussed by G. Aquilecchia in an article entitled 'U e non-U nell' italiano parlato' which appeared in *Questioni* (vol. V, pp. 4–11). This complexity is not rendered easier by the fact that—as has often been said—'All Italians are bilingual; they speak the *lingua nazionale* and also their local dialect'. But there *are* U/non-U differences. The non-U are fonder of euphemisms than the U; they say *impedito* (meaning 'handicapped') whereas the U say *paralitico* (meaning 'paralysed'). The U use the word *film* (meaning 'movie'); the Italian word for it, *pellicola*, is non-U. Do not ask for a *cognacchino*; just say *cognac*, in which the U now put the accent on the first syllable, though they used to put it on the second. And, if you get it, do not say *cin cin*, an expression introduced into non-U Italian during the Second World War—the Italians apparently thought that *Chin-Chin!* was what the English said when drinking. U for 'spectacles' is *occhiali*, non-U *lenti*, which means 'lenses'. The word *anteguerra*—as in *prezzi anteguerra* meaning 'pre-War, i.e. low prices'—is especially non-U. The Italian non-U seem to have a peculiar trick of pronunciation; they tend to withdraw the accent by one syllable and say, for instance, *persuàdere* instead of *persuadère*.

Portuguese and the Scandinavian languages have absolutely no trace of U and non-U. The same is true of Spanish. In Spain a duchess and a chambermaid—there are plenty of both—speak exactly the same.

German, too, has little. To speak with a dialect accent is certainly not non-U. Admittedly to say *Mahlzeit!* (which means 'meal-time') before sitting down to a meal, or even when meeting someone in the street, is exclusively working-class. However, at one time, one particular German class did have a special way of talking. This class was that of the Prussian officers. Those who know German well will appreciate the significance of the following—from *Simplicissimus*, the nearest thing the Germans have to *Punch*, in 1897: Two men in a Turkish bath, one an officer wearing a monocle but nothing else. In the caption, the other man says: 'Herr Lieutenant tragen das Monocle im Bad?' [which means 'The Lieutenant wears his monocle in the bath?'] and the officer's reply, full of linguistic indicators, is 'Äh, befürchte sonst für Civilisten jehalten zu werden' [which means 'Well!—otherwise I'd be afraid of being thought to be a civilian'].

In England, if a U-person discusses U and non-U, the worst that can happen to him is that he may be publicly castigated as an appalling snob. In Russia, however—to judge from academic gossip seeping out from there—such discussion might have very serious consequences. It is therefore not surprising that class-distinction as expressed in speech is simply not discussed at all in the Russian literature. In the 1968 edition of R. I. Avanesov's *Russkoe literaturnoe proiznoshenie*,[1] the author has quite a bit to say on the pronunciations that mark out the actor, the academic and the intellectually pretentious person. But he has only one single remark about class-distinction in Language; at page 20 he refers (I translate) to 'the tendency of certain social circles to fence themselves off from the general national language by their "class" jargons (example, the nobility in Czarist Russia)'. This remark could hardly offend anyone in Russia. Unfortunately Avanesov gives no examples of Russian 'noble's jargon' and, at this distance of time, it might be difficult to collect any. But a careful reading of the pre-Revolution novels might yield something. However, despite this conspiracy of silence, it is rumoured that there *are* linguistic class-distinctions in Russia. It seems that, whereas in the immediately post-Revolution and Stalinist periods, it was, naturally, correct to talk in a very proletarian fashion, there is now some sort of return to a 'good' Russian—whatever exactly that may mean.

In a sense it is in Japanese that U and non-U finds its apo-

[1] Surely a rather carefully chosen title—it means 'Russian literary pronunciation'.

theosis—in the form of the language which is called *keigo*. This term is usually translated as 'Respect Language'. For a foreigner, it is undoubtedly very complex and very difficult. Those who know some Japanese will find Professor P. G. O'Neill's *Programmed course on Respect Language in Modern Japanese* exceedingly helpful; I quote and take examples from it here. 'Respect language means the special style of speech or writing used in Japanese to show respect to persons . . . Respect can be shown both to the person one is talking to and to the person one is talking about . . . Women . . . use respect language more consistently and extensively than other people'. It is particularly used by a younger to an older person. Sometimes the difference between respect language and normal language merely consists in a difference between words; the following are examples—I give the respect form first: *kata* and *hito*, both meaning 'person'; *donata* and *dare*, both meaning 'who?'; *yoroshii* and *ii*, both meaning 'good'. Often respect is expressed by means of prefixes and/or suffixes; thus *nee* means 'elder sister'; *nee-san* and *o-nee-san* are respect forms of the word. The suffix -*sama* denotes more than usual respect, as in *Kootaishi-sama* meaning 'the Crown Prince'. Sometimes women add the respect prefix *o-* to peculiar things, as in *o-toiretto*, meaning 'lavatory', in which the latter part of the word is the English word *toilet*. For the learner, the real horrors of the Respect Language lie in the Japanese equivalents of the English verb and adjective. In Japanese there also exists something that is, in a way, the opposite of Respect Language. This is obsequious language—a form in which the speaker depreciates himself.[1]

In Dutch the U/non-U distinction is well evidenced. This is not surprising, for after all, Holland is not a country which can be said to be entirely non-snobbish. The subject has been studied in detail in an anonymous article in *Onze Taal*, June–July 1962. The article is entitled 'Joe en nonjoe'.[2] The author starts by

[1] Something very similar to the Japanese Respect Language is found in Indonesian languages such as Javanese.

[2] The Dutch cannot use my 'U' in this context, because, in Dutch, *U*

23

pointing out that the whole subject is considered highly taboo, by both U and non-U. In addressing envelopes the Dutch have similar worries to the English—when do you put *Weledel*—which means, literally, 'very noble'—before a man's name, and when *Weledelgestreng*, which means, literally, 'very noble and valiant'? The spoken language affords a large number of examples. One really is curious: in addressing a married woman, it is non-U to use her surname (as *mevrouw Jansen*), but U just to say *mevrouw*. With men it is just the opposite: *meneer Jansen* is U, but plain *meneer* is non-U. Sometimes a foreign word is non-U; thus to say the English *sorry* is non-U for *het spijt me*, and *mijn excuses* is non-U for *verontschuldiging*. The French *visite* is non-U for *bezoek*. But *auto* meaning 'car' is U, while the native *wagen* is non-U. Many of the Dutch examples are curiously like the English; *griep hebben* means 'to have influenza' but to use the definite article, *de*, and say *de griep hebben* 'to have the influenza', is non-U.

In Welsh, the U/non-U position is curious. In the spoken language the difference virtually does not appear. There is certainly a difference between colloquial Welsh and 'public' Welsh—this being essentially the Welsh of the pulpit—but this has nothing to do with class. However, in literary Welsh there are distinctions comparable to our U and non-U. In the nineteenth century Welsh suffered greatly from anglicisms and from words invented by quack lexicographers, and these gradually came to be felt as non-U. Words so coined such as *cerbydres* meaning 'train' (literally 'vehicle-series') were avoided. Often a return to medieval Welsh was made; thus the old word *odid*, which means 'rarity', came to be used to mean 'unlikely'. But now such medievalisms are, in turn, felt to be non-U. Naturally a particular loathing has been and is felt for English influence on the language. This does not, however, mean an aversion to borrowed words; there is nothing non-U about the word *potel* meaning 'bottle'. It is rather the literal translation of whole

means 'you'. *Joe* is a coined word, pronounced the same as *U* (or *you*) is in English.

English expressions that is felt to be particularly bad. Recently, the use of real dialect words in writing has become very fashionable and U—such as *Sianiflewog* meaning 'hairy caterpillar'— *Siani* is our *Jane* and *flewog* means 'hairy'—so the word literally means 'hairy Jane'.[1]

For Finland we have an interesting source. M. Sadeniemi reviewed (in Finnish) my original article 'U and non-U' (see page 10, above) in the 1955 volume of the periodical *Virittäjä* (pp. 201–3), and, incidentally, discussed the Finnish situation. A distinction between U and non-U really only manifests itself as a distinction between educated and uneducated. This chiefly appears in the pronunciation of foreign words. Thus it is not educated to say *lonkitudi* instead of *longitudi* for 'longitude'. Since Swedish is the first foreign language learnt by Finnish-speaking Finns, lack of education is particularly likely to appear in the mispronunciation of Swedish words. The Swedes make use of the English word *journalist* but they pronounce it with initial [sh]. The Finns have taken the word over from the Swedes, and the correct Finnish form is *shurnalisti*. But [sh] is a difficult sound for Finns, so many say *surnalisti* (with [s] instead of [sh]). This is considered bad. Oddly enough considerable latitude in the pronunciation of French words is beginning to be allowed and, for instance, to say *prestiisi*, in which [s] is substituted for the [zh] of French *prestige*, is now permitted, though it would not have been some years ago. In native Finnish, Mr. Sadeniemi particularly frowns on the use of the children's *isi* for *isä* (which is the Finnish for 'father'). Is this the sole example of Finnish baby-talk? When I was in Finland learning Finnish in 1934, I do not remember any silly Finnish girls using baby-talk, though it, with its companion, pseudo-Cockney, was not unknown to silly English girls of the period—*ickle dlinkie* for *little drink*, or *Cor! He ain't 'arf barmy!*, respectively.

Is there U and non-U in exotic languages? I only know one, Tahitian, and there is certainly nothing of the kind there. There

[1] From information kindly placed at my disposal by Professor T. J. Morgan, University College of Swansea.

is nothing either U or non-U, for instance, about the word *pua'ahorofenua* which actually means 'horse' though literally 'pig that runs over the country'. In many exotic languages, however, certain forms of speech are confined to certain members of the community, for instance, old women or children. Many examples are to be found among the two thousand or so languages of the American continent.

LIST OF WORDS AND NAMES

AARHUS, Denmark: [awr-hoos], first syllable the same as *or* before a vowel (with R sounded), second syllable to rhyme with *moose*.

ABADAN, Iran: [ab-ə-dan], accent on third syllable.

ABBEVILLE, town in France, known from the 1914–18 War: [ab-veel], first syllable to rhyme with *cab*, second the same as *veal*.

ABDOMEN: [ab-doh-men], accent on second syllable. OR [ab-də-mən], accent on first syllable.

ABERAVON, Wales: [ab-ə-rav-ən], third syllable to rhyme with *have*. NOT [ab-ə-rayv-ən], last two syllables the same as *raven*.

ABERAYRON, Wales: [ab-ə-reə-rən], last two syllables to rhyme with *Aaron*.

ABERDOVEY, Wales: [ab-ə-dʌv-i], third syllable the same as *dove*.

ABERGAVENNY: pronounced as spelt [ab-ə-gə-ven-i], five syllables, accent on the fourth, when it is the town in Monmouth, but [ab-ə-gen-i], four syllables, no V, when it is the title of a peer.

ABERNETHY, Scotch surname: [ab-ə-neth-i], third syllable to rhyme with *breath*. NOT [ab-ə-neeth-i], third syllable rhyming with *heath*.

27

ABERTILLERY, Monmouth: [ab-ə-til-ɛ̯ə-ri], last two syllables to rhyme with *hairy*. OR [ab-ə-til-e̯e̯ə-ri], last two syllables the same as *eerie*.

ABERYSTWYTH, Wales: [ab-ə-rist-with], third syllable the same as *wrist*. OR [ab-ə-rʌst-with], third syllable the same as *rust*.

ABHOR: (əb-haw], H sounded, second syllable the same as *hoar*. [əb-aw], no H, is faintly parsonical. Similarly ABHORRENCE, ABHORRENT, with or without H.

ABSINTH. To-day the French pronunciation (of *absinthe*) is usual.

ABSOLVE: [ab-zolv]. NOT [ab-zohlv]; this last is usually non-U, but can be parsonical.

ABSURD: [ab-surd]; but [ab-zurd] is also known among both U and non-U speakers.

ABU QIR, Egypt, known from the Battle of Aboukir Bay (1798): [ə-book-yə], accent on second syllable. NOT [ab-u-kee̯ə], accent on third syllable—a pronunciation which is, however, more like the Arabic.

ACACIA: [ə-kays-yə], middle syllable the same as *case*, is perhaps more usual than [ə-kaysh-ə], last two syllables to rhyme with *geisha*.

ACCOLADE: [ak-ə-lahd], third syllable the same as *lard*, is more usual than [ak-ə-layd], third syllable the same as *laid*.

ACCOMPLICE: [ə-kʌm-plis], second syllable the same as *come*. NOT [ə-kom-plis], second syllable rhyming with *Tom*.

28

ACCOMPLISH: [ə-kʌm-plish], second syllable the same as *come*. OR [ə-kom-plish], second syllable to rhyme with *Tom*.

ACCRA, Ghana: [ə-krah], accent on second syllable.

ACKNOWLEDGE: [ək-nol-ij], second syllable to rhyme with *doll*. NOT [ək-nohl-ij], second syllable rhyming with *dole*.

ACOUSTICS: [ə-kus-tiks], second syllable to rhyme with *puss*. OR [ə-koos-tiks], second syllable to rhyme with *moose*. OR [ə-kous-tiks], second syllable to rhyme with *mouse*.

ACRE, town in Israel, well known in the Crusades: [ay-kə], the same as *acre* meaning 'a measure of land'.

ACROSS: [ə-kraws], second syllable to rhyme with *force*. OR [ə-kros], second syllable to rhyme with *Ross*.

ACTUAL: [ak-chʊ-əl], [kch] as *ckch* of *deck-chair*; or [ak-tyʊ-əl]. NOT [ak-shəl], [ksh] as *cks* of *cocksure*.

ACTUALLY: [ak-chʊ-li], [ak-tyʊ-li]. NOT [ak-shə-li]. The pronunciation [ak-shli], two syllables, appears among U, and perhaps also non-U schoolboys.

ADDIS ABABA, Ethiopia: [a-dis a-bə-bə]. NOT [a-dis ə-bah-bə], last two syllables the same as *barber*.

ADELINE, Christian name: [ad-ə-leen], last syllable the same as *lean*. NOT [ad-ə-lɛin], last syllable the same as *line*.

ADEPT, noun: [ad-ept], accent on first syllable; the adjective usually has this same accentuation nowadays, though [ə-dept], accent on second syllable, is also known.

ADHERENT: [ad-heeə-rənt], second syllable the same as *hear*. NOT [ad-he-rənt], last two syllables rhyming with *errant*.

29

ADIEU: [ə-dyo͟o], second syllable the same as *dew*. OR in the French way.

ADULT: [a͟d-ʌlt], accent on first syllable. OR [ə-dʌlt], accent on second.

ADUR, Sussex river: [a͟yd-ə], to rhyme with *wader*. NOT [a͟d-ə], the same as *adder*.

ADVANCE: [əd-va͟hns], second syllable to rhyme with *France*. NOT [əd-va͟ns], second syllable rhyming with *manse*.

ADVERTISEMENT: [əd-vu͟rt-iz-mənt], accent on second syllable. NOT [ad-vurt-ɡi͟z-mənt], accent on third.

AESCHYLUS: [e͟esk-yʋ-ləs].

AESTHETIC: [ees-the͟t-ik], second syllable to rhyme with *bet*. NOT [ees-the͟et-ik], second syllable rhyming with *beat*.

AFGHANISTAN: [af-ɡa͟n-is-tan], last syllable the same as *tan*. OR [af-ɡa͟n-is-tahn], last syllable the same as *tarn*.

AFTER: [a͟hf-tə], first syllable to rhyme with *scarf*. NOT [a͟f-tə], first syllable rhyming with *gaff*.

AFTERMATH: [a͟hf-tə-math], last syllable to rhyme with *hath*, is better than [a͟hf-tə-mahth], last syllable rhyming with *hearth*.

AFTERNOON: [ahf-tə-no͟on], accent on last syllable. NOT [a͟hf-tə-noon], accent on first syllable. It is from this latter pronunciation that the non-U abbreviation *after*, meaning 'afternoon', derives.

AGAIN: [ə-ɡa͟yn], second syllable to rhyme with *pain*. OR [ə-ɡe͟n], second syllable to rhyme with *pen*. Similarly AGAINST.

30

AGREEABLE. Strictly [ə-greeə-bəl], but [ə-grib-əl], last two syllables to rhyme with *dribble*, is often heard.

AIDE-DE-CAMP. The French pronunciation is normal.

AITHNE, Irish Christian name: [eth-ni]; so the name is often spelt *Ethne*.

ALABAMA. The American pronunciation is [al-ə-bam-ə], last two syllables to rhyme with *hammer*; but some Englishmen say [al-ə-bahm-ə], last two syllables to rhyme with *calmer*.

ALABASTER: [a-lə-bahs-tə], third syllable to rhyme with *farce*. NOT [a-lə-bas-tə], third syllable rhyming with *gas*.

À LA MODE, best known to-day in *apple-pie à la mode*, which means 'apple tart with ice-cream': [ah-lah-mohd]. To use the French pronunciation is pedantic or affected.

ÅLAND *Islands*: [oh-lənd], to rhyme with *Poland*.

ALAS: [ə-lahs], second syllable to rhyme with *sparse*; [ə-las], second syllable to rhyme with *gas*, is old-fashioned.

ALDEBARAN, star-name. Astronomers call it [al-deb-ə-rən], accent on second syllable. NOT [al-də-beə-rən] or [al-də-bah-rən], accent on third syllable; or [al-di-bə-ran], accent on fourth.

ALDEBURGH, Suffolk: [awld-bə-rə], last part the same as that of *Edinburgh*. NOT [awl-di-burg].

ALDERMASTON, Berkshire. The local pronunciation is [awl-də-mas-tən], third syllable to rhyme with *gas*. But many people call it [awl-də-mahs-tən], third syllable to rhyme with *farce*.

31

ALETHEA, Christian name: [al-ə-thęęə], accent on last syllable. NOT [ə-lęęth-i-yə], accent on second.

ALEUTIAN *Islands*: [ə-lǫǫ-shən]. OR [ə-lyǫǫ-shən], three syllables; surprisingly, not [al-i-yǫǫ-shən], four syllables, which would be more correct, because the Russian for *Aleut*— a person who lives there—is *aleut* not *alyut*.

ALGIERS: [al-jęęəz], accent on second syllable. NOT [al-jeeəz], accent on first.

ALLAHABAD, India: [al-ə-hə-bad], accent on last syllable.

ALLIES: [al-ɛiz], accent on first syllable. But [əl-ɛiz], accent on second syllable, was used in the 1914–18 War.

ALLOA, Scotland: [al-oh-ə], accent on first syllable.

ALMANAC: [awl-mə-nak], first syllable the same as *all*. NOT [ol-mə-nak], first syllable rhyming with *doll*; or [al-mə-nak], first syllable rhyming with *pal*.

ALMOST: [awl-mohst], first syllable the same as *all*. NOT [ol-mohst], first syllable rhyming with *doll*.

ALNMOUTH, Northumberland: [ayl-məth], no N, but this pronunciation is virtually obsolete. [yęl-məth] is quite obsolete. To-day most people call it [ahn-məth], first syllable to rhyme with *barn*, or [al-ən-mouth], three syllables.

ALNWICK, Northumberland: [an-ik], to rhyme with *panic*.

ALREADY: [awl-ręd-i], first syllable the same as *all*. OR [ol-ręd-i], first syllable to rhyme with *doll*.

32

ALSO: [a̲wl-soh], first syllable the same as *all*. NOT [o̲l-soh], first syllable rhyming with *doll*.

ALTAR and ALTER are, by everyone, pronounced the same: [a̲wl-tə], first syllable the same as *all*. NOT [o̲l-tə], first syllable rhyming with *doll*.

ALTERNATE. Accent on second syllable when it is an adjective, on the first when it is a verb. Adjective: [awl-tu̲r-nit]; verb: [a̲wl-tə-nayt], first syllable the same as *all*. NOT [ol-tu̲r-nit], [o̲l-tə-nayt], first syllable rhyming with *doll*. ALTERNATING, as in *alternating current*, like the verb: [a̲wl-tə-nay-ting]. NOT [o̲l-tə-nay-ting].

ALTHOUGH: [awl-dho̲h̲], first syllable the same as *all*. OR [ol-dho̲h̲], first syllable to rhyme with *doll*.

ALTITUDE: [a̲l-ti-tyood], first syllable to rhyme with *pal*. The pronunciation [a̲wl-ti-tyood], first syllable the same as *all*, is also known.

ALTOGETHER: [awl-tə-ge̲dh-ə], first syllable the same as *all*. OR [ol-tə-ge̲dh-ə], first syllable to rhyme with *doll*.

ALTRINCHAM, Cheshire: [a̲wl-tring-əm], second syllable to rhyme with *ring*. NOT [a̲wl-trinch-əm], second syllable rhyming with *pinch*.

ALUMINIUM: [a-lʋ-mi̲n-yəm], accent on third syllable. The American for it is *aluminum*, pronounced [ə-lo̲o-min-əm], accent on second syllable. For both Englishmen and Americans the well-known tongue-twister is difficult: *Are you copperbottoming that boat, my good man?—No, I'm aluminiuming it, ma'am.*

ALWAYS: [a̲wl-wiz], first syllable the same as *all*. OR [o̲l-wiz], first syllable to rhyme with *doll*.

33

AMATEUR: [a̱m-ə-tur]. The pronunciations [a̱m-ə-tooə], [a̱m-ə-chooə], [a̱m-ə-chə] are old-fashioned.

AMEN: [ah-me̱n], first syllable to rhyme with *star*. [ay-me̱n], first syllable to rhyme with *stay*, is also possible.

AMICABLE: [a̱m-ik-ə-bəl], accent on first syllable. NOT [am-i̱k-ə-bəl], accent on second.

AMUCK, that is, AMOK; this last is a Malay word meaning 'a furious attack'. The correct pronunciation is [a̱h-mok], accent on the first syllable, and this pronunciation is used technically, as in *amok-running*. Generally, however, the word is pronounced [ə-mʌk], accent on second syllable, and therefore written *amuck*, as in *to run amuck*.

ANALOGOUS: [ə-na̱l-ə-gəs], with [g] in *gun*. But the word is often pronounced [ə-na̱l-ə-jəs], with [j] in *jet*; this is because *analogy* is pronounced with [j] in *jet*: [ə-na̱l-ə-ji].

ANASTASIA, Christian name: [an-ə-sta̱yz-yə], third syllable the same as *stays*. NOT [an-ə-sta̱hz-yə], third syllable the same as *stars*.

ANCESTOR: [a̱n-ses-tə], first syllable to rhyme with *tan*. NOT [a̱hn-ses-tə], first syllable rhyming with *tarn*.

ANCHOVY: [a̱n-chə-vi], accent on first syllable. OR [an-cho̱h-vi], accent on second.

ANDOVER, Hampshire: [a̱n-do-və], accent on first syllable. NOT [a̱n-do̱h-və], rhyming with *hand over*.

ANEURIN, Welsh Christian name: [ə-ne̱i-rin], second syllable the same as *nigh*. Hence the abbreviation *Nye*.

34

ANGER: [ang-gə]. OR [eng-gə].

ANGMERING, Sussex: [ang-mə-ring], accent on first syllable.

ANKARA, Turkey: [ang-kə-rə], accent on first syllable. It used to be called ANGORA and, in *Angora rabbit*, this is pronounced [ang-gaw-rə], accent on second syllable.

ANKETELL, surname: [ang-kət-el], accent on last syllable.

ANSWER: [ahn-sə], first syllable to rhyme with *France*. NOT [ans-ə], first syllable rhyming with *manse*.

ANT: [ant], to rhyme with *cant*. NOT [ahnt], rhyming with *can't*.

ANTARCTIC: [ant-ahk-tik], first C sounded. NOT [ant-ah-tik], without first C.

ANTHEA, Christian name: [an-thi-yə], accent on first syllable. NOT [an-thee-yə], accent on second.

ANTIGUA, West Indies; there, it is pronounced [an-teeg-ə], three syllables. But, in England, it is usually called [an-tig-yʊ-ə], four syllables. This pronunciation is needed for a limerick in which the last three syllables of the word rhyme with [fig-yʊ-ə], facetious pronunciation of *figure*.

ANTIQUARY: [ant-i-kwer-i], accent on first syllable. NOT [an-tik-wer-i], accent on second.

ANTROBUS, surname: [an-trə-bəs], accent on first syllable. NOT [an-troh-bəs], accent on the second, though this pronunciation can be heard in the United States.

35

APHRODISIAC: [af-ro-dĭz-yak], third syllable to rhyme with *whizz*. OR [af-ro-dẹiz-yak], third syllable to rhyme with *wise*.

APPARATUS: [ap-ə-rạyt-əs], third syllable the same as *rate*. NOT [ap-ə-raht-əs], third syllable rhyming with *dart*; or [ap-ə-rạt-əs], third syllable the same as *rat*. The plural is *apparatuses*, not the bad Latin *apparati*, still less the correct Latin *apparatūs*, which last would yield an English pronunciation [ap-ə-rạyt-tyoos], last syllable the same as the second syllable of *obtuse*.

APPARENTLY: [ə-pẹə-rənt-li], middle part the same as *parent*; or [ə-pạ-rənt-li], middle part to rhyme with *arrant*. NOT [ə-pah-rənt-li], second syllable the same as *par*.

APPLICABLE: [ạp-lik-ə-bəl], accent on first syllable. NOT [əp-lĭk-ə-bəl], accent on second.

AQUATIC: [ə-kwạt-ik], second syllable to rhyme with *rat*. NOT [ə-kwọt-ik], second syllable rhyming with *rot*.

ARBUCKLE, surname: [ạh-bʌk-əl], accent on first syllable.

ARBUTHNOT, surname: [ah-bʌth-not], accent on second syllable.

ARCTIC: [ạhk-tik], first C sounded. NOT [ạh-tik], without first C.

ARDAGH, Irish surname: [ạhd-ə], the same as *ardour*.

ARDRISHAIG, Scotland: [ah-drĭsh-ayg], accent on second syllable.

ARISTOCRAT: [ạr-is-tək-rat], accent on first syllable. NOT [ə-rĭs-tək-rat], accent on second.

ARKANSAS, U.S.A.: [ah-kan-səs], accent on second syllable, final S sounded. But the American pronunciation is [ah-kən-saw], accent on first syllable, last syllable the same as *saw*—no final S.

ARMAGH, Ireland: [ah-mah], accent on second syllable.

ARMENTIÈRES, France. In the 1914–18 War the pronunciation was [ah-mən-teeəz], last syllable to rhyme with *fears*, the first and third syllables being equally stressed. The name is known in the song of the period, *Mademoiselle from Armentières.*

ARMISTICE: [ahm-is-tis], accent on first syllable. NOT [ahm-is-tis], accent on second.

ARTISAN: [ah-tiz-an], accent on last syllable. NOT [ah-tiz-ən], accent on first.

ARUNDEL, Sussex: [ar-ən-dəl], accent on first syllable. NOT [ə-rʌn-dəl], accent on second.

ARYAN, term formerly used of certain peoples and their languages, and ARIAN (of the Heresy) are both pronounced in the same way: [eə-ryən], first syllable to rhyme with *care*. NOT [ah-ryən], first syllable to rhyme with *car*.

*Ashby-de-la-*ZOUCH, Leicestershire: [zooch], to rhyme with *mooch*. NOT [zoosh], to rhyme with *douche*, or [zouch], to rhyme with *couch*; or [zoush]. But the village of *Zouch*, about twelve miles East of the town, is pronounced [zoch], to rhyme with *Scotch.*

ASIA: [aysh-ə], to rhyme with *geisha*; [ayzh-ə], first syllable to rhyme with *beige*, is, however, also known—? old-fashioned U. Similarly ASIATIC, with [sh] or [zh].

ASK: [ahsk]. NOT [ask]. The pronunciation [aks], the same as *axe*, is dialectal. Something like [ɛəsk] is very old-fashioned U.

ASPECT: [as-pekt], first syllable to rhyme with *gas*. NOT [ahs-pekt], first syllable rhyming with *farce*.

ASPHALT: [as-felt], first syllable to rhyme with *gas*, second the same as *felt*; or [as-falt]. NOT [ahs-felt] or [ahs-falt], first syllable rhyming with *farce*.

ASPIRANT: [as-pi-rənt], accent on first syllable, which rhymes with *gas*. NOT [əs-pɛir-ənt], accent on second.

ASS. This word is not used in England in its true sense, except in the Bible (e.g. *Go into the village over against you, and straightway ye shall find an ass tied*, Matthew xxi. 2) and in Zoology. *Donkey*—or the facetious *moke*—are, in England, used instead. But in Ireland *ass* is used to mean 'donkey', and is pronounced [as], to rhyme with *gas*. In the transferred use, *silly ass*, etc., those who pronounce *pass* as [pahs], to rhyme with *farce*, do not usually say [ahs]; they say [as], because [ahs] is the pronunciation of *arse*. Some old-fashioned U-speakers, who say [pahs], do, however, also say [ahs]. As a verb—*stop assing about*, meaning 'stop fooling about', *ass* is, however, pronounced [ahs]; this verb-idiom seems to be an old-fashioned U one. It may be noted here that Americans, for some reason, feel it is less 'rude' to spell the word *arse*, A,S,S; as in the American phrase *ass over tea-kettle*, meaning 'head over heels', used by an astronaut to an English Sunday newspaper reporter.

ASSUME: [ə-syoom], second syllable to rhyme with *fume*; [ə-soom], second syllable to rhyme with *doom* is also known; [ə-shoom], is, essentially, a drunk's pronunciation.

38

ASTRAKHAN, Russia: [as-trə-ka̲hn], last syllable to rhyme with *barn*. But the pseudo-fur is usually called [as-trə-ka̲n], last syllable to rhyme with *ban*.

ATE (past tense of *eat*): [et], to rhyme with *wet*. NOT [ayt], rhyming with *wait*.

ATHLONE, Ireland: [əth-lo̲hn], accent on second syllable.

ATHOLL, Scotland: [a̲th-ol].

AUCHINLECK, town in Scotland, and surname: once [a̲f-lik], first syllable to rhyme with *gaff*, but now pronounced [a̲wk-in-lek], as spelt, by many. Hence the nickname *The Auk* for the Second War general of that name.

AUCHTERMUCHTY, Scotland: [o̲k-tə-mʌk-ti], the first and third syllables being equally stressed, and, strictly, with Scotch *ch* in *loch* for the two [k]-sounds. It is said that no U-person has ever been there, so that there is no U-pronunciation. The English parallel would thus, once, have been *Wigan*.

Auld lang SYNE: [sɛin], the same as *sign*. NOT [zɛin], the same as the second syllable of *design*.

AUNT: [ahnt], to rhyme with *can't*. NOT [ant], rhyming with *cant*. AUNTIE pronounced [a̲nt-i], the same as *ante* (in Poker), is very non-U.

AU REVOIR: [o̲h rəv-wa̲h]. The pronunciation [o̲h rə-vo̲i-yə] is a facetious U aping of a supposed non-U pronunciation, which, possibly, never existed.

AUSTRALIA: [os-tra̲y-lyə], first syllable to rhyme with *Ross*. NOT [aws-tra̲y-lyə], first syllable rhyming with *force*. Many Australians say [os-trɛ̲i-lyə], second syllable the same as *try*.

Their language, *Australian*—that is, Australian English, they often call [strɛin], one syllable, to rhyme with *fine*.

AUSTRIA: [ọs-tryə], first syllable to rhyme with *Ross*. [aws-tryə], first syllable to rhyme with *force*, is old-fashioned and was used in the 1914–18 War. Similarly AUSTRO–HUNGARIAN.

AVIEMORE, Scotland: [av-i-maw], accent on last syllable, first to rhyme with *have*. NOT [ayv-i-maw], accent on first syllable rhyming with *brave*.

AZERBAIJAN, U.S.S.R.: [az-ə-bg̣ij-ən], accent on third syllable, which rhymes with the second syllable of *Elijah*.

AZORES: [ə-zawz], two syllables. But, in the first line of Tennyson's poem *The Revenge*—'At Flores in the Azores Sir Richard Grenville lay', the word is presumably pronounced [ə-zaw-riz], three syllables.

AZURE: [azh-ə], accent on first syllable; or [ay-zhə], to rhyme with some people's pronunciation of *Asia*. NOT [ə-zyaw], accent on second.

BACCARAT: [bak-ə-rah], no T. NOT [bak-ə-rat], with T.

BACKGAMMON: [bak-gam-ən], the first and second syllables being equally stressed—just as if it were the two words as spelt. The pronunciation [bə-gam-ən], no CK, and accent on second syllable, is old-fashioned.

BACKWATER, noun: [bak-waw-tə], accent on first syllable. But the expression *to* BACK WATER (rowing) is [bak-waw-tə], the first two syllables being equally stressed.

BACUP, Lancashire: [bayk-əp], first syllable the same as *bake*. NOT (bak-əp], first syllable the same as *back*.

BAGEHOT, surname: [bag-ət], to rhyme with *maggot*; but the pronunciation [baj-ət], first syllable the same as *badge*, is sometimes used.

BALA, lake in Wales: [bal-ə], first syllable to rhyme with *pal*. NOT [bahl-ə], first syllable rhyming with *marl*.

BALAKLAVA, Russia, known from the Crimean War—and, until recently, there was the knitted object called a *Balaclava helmet*: [bal-ə-klah-və], accent on third syllable, which rhymes with *far*.

BALCHIN, surname: [bawl-chin], first syllable the same as *ball*, second the same as *chin*. NOT [bal-chin], first syllable rhyming with *pal*, or [bol-chin], first syllable rhyming with *doll*, or [bawl-kin], [bal-kin], [bol-kin], second syllable the same as *kin*.

BALCONY: [bal-kə-ni], accent on first syllable; the pronunciation [bal-kohn-i], accent on second syllable, once acceptable, would to-day seem uneducated.

BALKANS: [bawl-kənz], first syllable the same as *ball*. NOT [bol-kənz], first syllable rhyming with *doll*.

BALTIC: [bawl-tik]. NOT [bol-tik].

BALLATER, Scotland: [bal-ə-tə], accent on first syllable, which rhymes with *pal*.

BALLINGER, surname: [bal-in-jə]. NOT [bal-ing-gə].

BALLIOL *College*: [bayl-yəl], two syllables, accent on the first, which is the same as *bail*. There is an ancient joke, the raison

41

d'être of which is the deliberate confusion of *Balliol* with the Biblical *Belial*—pronounced [beel-yəl], two syllables, first to rhyme with *peel*. Doubtless the joke arose from expressions in the Bible such as *Thou man of Belial*, II Samuel xvi. 7. But both *Balliol* and *Belial* are mispronounced in an identical way—as [bə-lei-yəl], three syllables, accent on the second.

BALLOON: [bloon], one syllable, to rhyme with *soon*. OR [bə-loon], two syllables, to rhyme with *Walloon*.

BALQUHIDDER, Scotland: [bal-hwid-ə], but with Scotch *ch* in *loch* for the [h]-sound.

BANAL: [bə-nal], accent on the second syllable; [bay-nəl], accent on the first syllable is also known, and so, too, were [bahn-əl], first syllable the same as *barn*, and also [ban-ahl], accent on first syllable, second to rhyme with *marl*.

BANGOR, Wales: [bang-gə]. NOT the Welsh pronunciation.

BARBADOS: [bah-bay-dohz], last syllable the same as *doze*. OR [bah-bay-dos], last syllable the same as *doss*.

BARENTS *Sea*: [beə-rənts], to rhyme with *parents*. But sometimes [bar-ənts].

BARING, surname: [beə-ring], first syllable the same as *bear*. NOT [bah-ring], first syllable the same as *baa*.

BARONET: [ba-rə-net]. The pronunciation [ba-ro-neit]—that is, *baroknight*—is one attributed by the U to the non-U, who did probably use it.

BARRACLOUGH, surname: [ba-rə-clʌf], last syllable to rhyme with *stuff*. NOT [ba-rə-clou], last syllable rhyming with *cow*.

42

BARRICO, small barrel: pronounced [bray-kə], the same as *breaker*, in the Navy.

BASALT: [bays-awlt], accent on the first syllable. OR [bə-sawlt], accent on second.

BASK: [bahsk]. NOT [bask].

BASKERVILLE, surname: [bas-kə-vil], first syllable to rhyme with *gas*. NOT [bahs-kə-vil], first syllable rhyming with *farce*. The name is probably best known from the Sherlock Holmes story, *The Hound of the Baskervilles*.

BASKET: [bahs-kit], first syllable to rhyme with *farce*. NOT [bas-kit], first syllable rhyming with *gas*.

BASLE, Switzerland: [bahl], to rhyme with *marl*.

BASRA, Iraq: [baz-rə], first syllable to rhyme with *has*.

BASS. This is [bays], the same as *base*, when applied to a voice, but [bas], to rhyme with *gas*, when applied to a fish.

BASTARD. This is best known as a mild term of abuse, sometimes a term of semi-affection, applied to a person or thing, and it is then usually pronounced [bahs-təd], first syllable to rhyme with *farce*. When used more technically it is pronounced [bas-təd], first syllable to rhyme with *gas*, as in *William the Bastard*, an unkind name for William the Conqueror, or in the Sciences, as *bastard pimpernel, bastard limestone*.

BATH: [bahth], to rhyme with *hearth*. NOT [bath], rhyming with *hath*.

BATTERY. Normally [bat-ər-i], first syllable the same as *bat*. But, when referring to a battery of Artillery, some Army people pronounce the word [bet-ər-i], first syllable the same as *bet*, though other Army people consider this affected.

BAULK: [bawk], no L, to rhyme with *fork*. NOT [bolk], with L.

BAYREUTH, Germany, known from its Opera: [bay-roit], first syllable the same as *bay*. The name can also be pronounced in the German way.

BEACONSFIELD, Buckinghamshire: [bek-ənz-feeld], first syllable to rhyme with *neck*. NOT as spelt.

BEANO: [bee-noh], to rhyme with the town in America, *Reno*. Curzon is reported to have pronounced the word [bi-yah-noh], three syllables, accent on the second, in a speech, because he was unfamiliar with it.

BEAUCHAMP, surname: [bee-chəm], to rhyme with *teach 'em* (i.e. *teach them*).

BEAUCLERK, surname: [bouk-lee], without final K, the two syllables being equally stressed.

BEAUFORT, peer's title: [bohf-ət], first syllable to rhyme with *loaf*.

BEAUFOY, surname: [boh-foi], first syllable to rhyme with *hoe*.

BEAULIEU, Hampshire: [byoo-li], to rhyme with *newly*.

BEAUMONT, surname: [boh-mənt], first syllable to rhyme with *hoe*.

BEAUNE, wine-name: [bohn], to rhyme with *tone*.

44

BEAUTIFUL: [byọọ-ti-fʊl], three syllables; even when heavily stressed it should not be [bi-yọọ-ti-fʊl], four syllables.

BECHER, surname, best known from *Becher's Brook* (Grand National): [bẹẹ-chə], to rhyme with *teacher*.

BECHUANALAND: [bek-yʊ-wạhn-ə-land], first syllable to rhyme with *neck*, is more usual than [bech-yʊ-wạhn-ə-land], first syllable to rhyme with *stretch*.

BEHAN, Irish surname: [bẹẹ-yən], to rhyme with *pæan*. NOT [bi-hạn], accent on second syllable and with H.

BEIRUT, Lebanon: [bay-rọọt], accent on second syllable, first syllable the same as *bay*.

BELIZE, British Honduras: [bə-lẹẹz], accent on second syllable, which is the same as *lees*.

BELVOIR, name of a Hunt: [bẹẹ-və], the same as *beaver*. NOT as spelt.

BENIN, Nigeria: [be-nịn], accent on second syllable.

BEN NEVIS, Scotland: [bẹn-nẹẹv-is], the first and second syllables being equally stressed, and the second syllable rhyming with *reeve*. OR [bẹn-nẹv-is], second syllable to rhyme with *rev*.

BENTHAM, surname: [bẹn-təm], the same as *bent 'em* (i.e. *bent them*). NOT [bẹn-thəm], with second syllable the same as that of *anthem*.

BERET: [bẹr-ay], no T. NOT [bẹr-i], the same as *berry*; or [bẹr-et], with T.

BERING *Sea*: [bẹə-ring], the same as *bearing*. NOT [bẹẹə-ring], rhyming with *hearing*.

45

BERKELEY, London Square, name of a Hunt, etc.: [bahk-li], to rhyme with *darkly*. NOT [burk-li], first syllable rhyming with *work*. This latter, non-U, pronunciation is preserved in the non-U *berk* (=approximately, *twerp*), which is an abbreviation for *Berkeley Hunt*, rhyming slang for a well-known four-letter word. The American University, *Berkeley* in California, is pronounced in the non-U way.

BERKHAMSTED, Hertfordshire: [burk-həm-sted], accent on first syllable, which rhymes with *work*. NOT [bahk-həm-sted], first syllable the same as *bark*, or [burk-ham-sted], [bahk-ham-sted], the first two syllables being equally stressed.

BERKSHIRE: [bahk-shə], first syllable the same as *bark*. NOT [burk-shə], first syllable rhyming with *work*.

BERNAL, surname: [bur-nal] or [bə-nal], accent on second syllable.

BERNE, Switzerland: [burn], the same as *burn*. NOT the French pronunciation.

BERSERK: [bur-surk], accent on first syllable. NOT [bə-zurk] or [bə-surk], accent on the second.

BERTIE, peer's title: [bah-ti], to rhyme with *party*. NOT [bur-ti], the same as the Christian name *Bertie*, which latter was, it seems, once pronounced as the peer is now.

BERWICK, Northumberland: [ber-ik], to rhyme with *Eric*.

BESANT, surname: [bə-zant], accent on second syllable. NOT [bez-ənt], accent on first; or [bə-sant] or [bes-ənt] or [bee-sənt], with S.

BESOM. Both broom and woman can be either [beez-əm], first syllable to rhyme with *cheese*; or [bez-əm], first syllable to rhyme with *fez*.

BETELGEUSE, star-name: [bet-əl-jurz], last syllable the same as the first syllable of *jersey* and accent on the first syllable, which is the same as *bet*. NOT [bet-əl-gurz]; or [bet-əl-jurz], or [bet-əl-gurz], accent on last syllable. The pronunciation [beet-əl-joos], that is *betel-juice*, is presumably a navigators' joke.

BETHUNE, surname: [beet-ən], to rhyme with *Eton*. NOT [beth-oon], or [bet-oon], accent on second syllable.

BEVIS, Christian name: [beev-is], first syllable to rhyme with *leave*.

BICESTER, Oxfordshire: [bis-tə], to rhyme with *sister*. NOT [bɛi-sɛs-tə], three syllables, accent on second and first the same as *buy*.

BIDEFORD, Devon: [bid-i-fəd], three syllables.

BIKINI, atoll in the Marshall Islands, where there was an atomic test. It has given its name, for no very obvious reason, to an exiguous female garment: [bi-keen-i], accent on second syllable.

BILBAO, Spain: [bil-bay-yoh], as spelt. OR the Spanish pronunciation.

BILLERICAY, Essex: [bil-i-rik-i], first two syllables the same as *Billy*, last two to rhyme with *tricky*.

BIRMINGHAM, England: [bur-ming-əm], to rhyme with *perming 'em* (as in *I'm perming them*—of hair or football results). NOT [bur-ming-ham], last syllable the same as *ham*, the first and third syllables being equally stressed. This latter pronunciation is used by train-announcers for clarity's sake. The old pronunciation [brʌm-ə-jəm], spelt *Brummagem*, is no longer used, but its abbreviation *Brum*, to rhyme with *drum*, is used as a term of facetious endearment for Birmingham by those who live there. So also *Brummie*, one who comes from Birmingham. The Alabama *Birmingham* is, by most Americans, pronounced in the way that is, for Englishmen, non-U; but some Americans use the English U-pronunciation for it.

BISON: [bɛis-ən], first syllable to rhyme with *price*, is, at least in this country, more usual than [bɛiz-ən], first syllable to rhyme with *prize*. I am not sure of the status of [biz-ən], to rhyme with *prison*—is it an American jocular pronunciation?

BLACKGUARD: [blag-əd], accent on first syllable and no CK, to rhyme with *haggard*. To pronounce it as two separate words, that is [blak gahd], with CK, the two parts being equally stressed, as is sometimes done in America, would suggest something quite different to an Englishman.

BLASÉ: [blah-zay]; or [blah-zi], accent on first syllable. The French pronunciation would be affected.

BLENHEIM *Palace*: [blɛn-im], to rhyme with *denim*.

BLOEMFONTEIN, South Africa: [blʊm-fon-tayn], accent on first syllable. NOT [bloom-fon-tayn], first syllable the same as *bloom*, or [blʊm-fon-tayn], [bloom-fon-tayn], accent on second syllable.

BLOODY: [blʌdi], to rhyme with *muddy*. The pronunciation [bə-lʌd-i], three syllables, is a facetious one of the nineteen-twenties when, at least in print, the word was still faintly naughty.

BLOUNT, surname: usually [blʌnt], the same as *blunt*.

BLOUSE: [blouz], to rhyme with *browse*. The pronunciation [blooz], to rhyme with *bruise*, is old-fashioned U.

48

BOADICEA. Usually pronounced [bawd-ə-see-yə], four syllables, but, more pedantically, [boh-ə-də-see-yə], five.

BOATSWAIN: [bohs-ən], no T, no W; first syllable to rhyme with *dose*. NOT as spelt.

BODLEIAN *Library*: [bod-lee-yən], accent on second syllable. NOT [bod-li-yən], accent on first.

BOER: [baw], the same as *bore*. OR [booə], to rhyme with many people's pronunciation of *poor*.

BOGOTA, Colombia: [bog-o-tah], accent on last syllable; but many Englishmen pronounce it [bə-goh-tə], accent on the second.

BOLEYN, surname, particularly that of Anne, wife of Henry VIII: [bʊl-in], accent on first syllable, which is the same as *bull*. NOT [bo-lin], accent on second. In either pronunciation the second syllable rhymes with *tin*.

BOLINGBROKE, peer's title: [bol-ing-brʊk], first syllable to rhyme with *doll*. NOT [bohl-ing-brʊk], first syllable the same as *bowl*; or [bʊl-ing-brʊk], first syllable the same as *bull*. In any pronunciation the last syllable is the same as *brook*.

BOLLARD: [bol-əd], accent on first syllable. NOT [bə-lahd], accent on second.

BOMBARDIER. Normally [bom-bə-deeə], first syllable to rhyme with *Tom*. The pronunciation [bʌm-bə-deeə], first syllable the same as *bum*, is known in the Army. Until about 1900 the Army pronounced the word *bomb* the same as *bum*, but this pronunciation has now died out.

BOOK: [bʊk]. NOT [book].

BOOR: [baw], the same as *bore*. OR [booə]. *Boer, boor* and *bore* are thus pronounced the same by many people.

BORDIGHERA, Italy: [bawd-i-geeə-rə], last two syllables to rhyme with *hearer*. OR in the Italian way.

BOSPORUS, straits in Turkey: [bos-fə-rəs], to rhyme with *phosphorus*; but often as spelt.

Boston SPA, Yorkshire. Normally with the standard pronunciation of *Spa* as [spah], to rhyme with *car*; but the older pronunciation [spaw], to rhyme with *caw*, is still heard.

BOTTOME, surname. Correctly, [bot-əm], the same as *bottom*. But the pronunciation [bot-ohm], accent on second syllable, has been used to avoid the unpleasant association.

BOULEVARD: [bool-ə-vahd], with final D. To use the French pronunciation would be pedantic.

BOULOGNE: [bʊ-lohn], second syllable the same as *loan*; the older pronunciation [bʊ-loin], second syllable the same as *loin*, can still be heard. OR in the French way.

BOUQUET: [bʊk-ay], accent on second syllable. OR [bʊk-ay], accent on the first, which is the same as *book*. The pronunciation [bohk-ay], first syllable to rhyme with *oak*, accent on the second, is a facetious aping of the non-U by U-speakers, though this pronunciation may well have actually existed among the non-U.

BOURBON—especially as the name of a chocolate biscuit: [bawb-ən], first syllable to rhyme with *daub*. OR, in the French way. It is now smart to use the American pronunciation [bur-bən], to rhyme with *turban*, for the American whisky called this.

BOURCHIER, surname: [bouch-ə], first syllable to rhyme with *couch*.

BOURNEMOUTH: [bawn-məth], first syllable the same as *born*. OR [booən-mouth].

BOURNVILLE, Birmingham: [bawn-vil], accent on first syllable. But its inhabitants usually call it [bawn-vil], the two syllables being equally stressed.

BRABANT, Belgium: [brə-bant], accent on second syllable. NOT [brab-ənt], accent on first.

BRABOURNE, peer's title: [bray-bən], first syllable the same as *bray*. NOT [brab-ən], first syllable rhyming with *blab*; or [brə-bawn], accent on second syllable.

BRANCH: [brahnch]. NOT [branch].

BRASS: [brahs], to rhyme with *farce*. NOT [bras], to rhyme with *gas*. This latter pronunciation, used in the sense 'money', is felt to be something peculiarly North Country.

BRASSERIE. There seems to be no accepted pronunciation of this word. It can be pronounced in a frenchified way. If anglicised, the first syllable can be [brahs], to rhyme with *farce*, or [bras], to rhyme with *gas*; and the accent can be on the first or on the third syllable. There are thus $2 \times 2 = 4$ possible 'English' pronunciations: [brahs-ə-ri], [bras-ə-ri], [brahs-ə-ree], [bras-ə-ree].

BRASSIÈRE. A frenchified pronunciation is normal (though the French do not use this word for the thing—they prefer the peculiar euphemism *soutien-gorge*). Also [brah-syɛə]—hence the abbreviation [brah] *bra*—or [bras-yɛə], first syllable to rhyme with *gas*.

BRAZIL, Irish surname: [braz-il], accent on first syllable. NOT [brə-zil], the same as the country.

BRAZZAVILLE, French Congo: [braz-ə-vil], first syllable to rhyme with *has*. NOT [brats-ə-vil], first syllable rhyming with *cats*.

BREADALBANE, Scotland: [bred-awl-bin], second syllable the same as *all*, third the same as *bin*.

BRECHIN, Scotland: [bree-kin], to rhyme with *Wrekin*. NOT [brech-in], first syllable rhyming with *fetch*, or [breech-in], first syllable rhyming with *teach*.

BRIAR: [brah], the same as *bra*. OR [brɛiə], to rhyme with *higher*.

BRIDGEND, Wales: [brij-end], accent on second syllable.

BRISBANE: [briz-bən], to rhyme with *Lisbon*. NOT [briz-bayn], accent on second syllable.

BRNO, Czecho-Slovakia: pronounced [brə-no] by most Englishmen. The German name of the town, *Brünn*, which is easier for the English to pronounce, is, of course, no longer used.

BROCCOLI: [brok-ə-li]. NOT [brok-ə-lɛi], last syllable the same as *lie*.

BROMLEY, Kent: [brom-li], first syllable to rhyme with *Tom*. [brʌm-li], first syllable to rhyme with *drum*, is old-fashioned.

BROMPTON *Road*: [brʌmp-tən], first syllable to rhyme with *trump*. NOT [bromp-tən], first syllable rhyming with *romp*.

BROTH: [brawth], to rhyme with *forth*. OR [broth], to rhyme with *moth*.

BROUGH, surname: [brʌf], to rhyme with *stuff*.

BROUGHAM, peer's title: [brʊm], the same as *broom*.

BRUGES, Belgium: [broozh], to rhyme with *rouge*. NOT [brooj], rhyming with *stooge*. To use a pronunciation with the French vowel would be affected.

BRUNEI: [brọọn-i-yɛi], accent on first syllable, is probably more usual than [brʊ-na̱y-yi], accent on second, which is the same as *neigh*.

BRUNEL, surname: [brʊ-nẹl], accent on second syllable.

BRYHER, one of the Scilly Islands: [brɛiə], no H, to rhyme with *higher*.

BRYNMAWR, Breconshire: [brin-ma̱ẖ], second syllable to rhyme with *car*. Better known as the name of an American female college, when it is pronounced [brin-ma̱w], second syllable the same as *more*.

BUCCLEUCH, peer's title: [bə-klọọ], to rhyme with last part of *hullabaloo*.

BUCHAREST: [byoo-kə-rẹst], first syllable to rhyme with *new*. [boo-kə-rẹst], first syllable the same as *boo*, is essentially American.

BUDAPEST: [byoo-də-pẹst], first syllable to rhyme with *new*. [boo-də-pẹst], first syllable the same as *boo*, is essentially American.

BUENOS AIRES: [bwa̱y-nəs ɛə̱-riz]. The pronunciation [bo̱h-nəs ɛə̱-riz], first two syllables the same as *bonus*, is old-fashioned. An approximation to the Spanish pronunciation, [bwa̱y-nəs ɛi̱-riz], is also heard.

BUFFET meaning 'a bar with snacks': [bṵf-ay], no T. The pronunciation [bʌf-it], the same as *buffet* meaning 'a blow', is what the U think the non-U call it. Perhaps they do. They certainly also call it a [bʌf-i], to rhyme with *stuffy*.

BUG, river in Russia: [bʌg], the same as *bug*.

BUILTH *Wells*, Breconshire: [beelth]. OR [bilth], to rhyme with *filth*.

BUKHARA, U.S.S.R.: [bə-ka̱h-rə], accent on second syllable.

BULGARIA: [bʌl-gɛə̱-ri-yə], first syllable to rhyme with *dull*, second with *there*. NOT [bʊl-ga̱h-ri-yə], first syllable rhyming with *pull*, second with *car*; or [bʌl-ga̱h-ri-yə], or [bʊl-gɛə̱-ri-yə].

BULL'S-EYE, the sweet, or the centre of a target: [bṵlz-ɛi], accent on the first syllable. [bṵlz-ɛi̱], the two syllables being equally stressed, can only mean the eye of a bull. A child went into a Leeds sweet-shop and asked for bull's-eyes with this stressing and was received with a stare; the sweets are called *humbugs* in the North of England.

BUNGAY, Suffolk: [bʌng-gi]. NOT [bʌng-i].

BURNETT, surname: [bur-ne̱t], accent on second syllable. But, in hyphenated names, such as *Hodgson-Burnett*, often [bu̱rn-it], accent on first syllable.

BURNTISLAND, Scotland: [bu̱rnt-ɛi̱-lənd], as if it were *burnt* + *island*. NOT [bu̱rn-tis-lənd], accent on first syllable, second rhyming with *hiss*.

BUSINESS: [biz-nis], two syllables; [biz-i-nis], three syllables, is BUSYNESS, the state of being busy.

BUTCHER: [bu̞-chə]; the pronunciation [bʌ-chə], to rhyme with *such a* (as in *such a man*), is well known in the North of England.

BYZANTINE. The first syllable can be pronounced in two ways— to rhyme with *Liz* or *lies*; there are two possibilities as to the accent—on first or second syllable; and the third syllable can be pronounced in three ways—to rhyme with *sin, seen* or *sign*. Theoretically at least, there are thus $2 \times 2 \times 3 = 12$ ways of pronouncing the word: [biz-ən-tin], [biz-ən-teen], [biz-ən-tɛin], [biz-an-tin], [biz-an-teen], [biz-an-tɛin], [bɛiz-ən-tin], [bɛiz-ən-teen], [bɛiz-ən-tɛin], [bɛiz-an-tin], [bɛiz-an-teen], [bɛiz-an-tɛin].

CABARET: [kab-ə-ray], no T. NOT [kab-ər-et], with T.

CABOT, surname: [kab-ət], with T. NOT [kab-oh], without T.

CADELL, surname: [kə-del], accent on second syllable.

CADIZ: [kəd-iz], accent on second syllable.

CADOGAN, surname: [kə-dʌg-ən], accent on second syllable, which is the same as *dug*.

CADRE, Army: [kah̲-də], to rhyme with *harder*. NOT [kay-də], rhyming with *wader*, or the French pronunciation.

CAERNARVON: [kə-nah̲v-ən], accent on second syllable, which rhymes with *halve*.

CAFÉ: [kaf-ay], accent on first syllable; [kaf-i], to rhyme with *Taffy*, is also possible. NOT [kə-fay], accent on second

55

syllable. The pronunciation [kayf], to rhyme with *safe*, is considered so non-U as to be a joke. But, in fact, the non-U mostly say [kaf], to rhyme with *gaff*.

CAFFEINE: [kaf-een], two syllables. The more correct pronunciation [kaf-i-een], three syllables, would sound pedantic.

CAICOS *Islands*: [kay-kəs], to rhyme with *Wake us!*

CAIRO: [kah-roh], first syllable the same as *car*. OR [kεiə-roh], first part to rhyme with *higher*.

CAISSON, piece of underwater apparatus used in laying foundations: [kə-soon], accent on second syllable, to rhyme with *bassoon*. OR [kay-sən], accent on first syllable, to rhyme with *basin*.

CAITHNESS: [kayth-nεs], accent on second syllable.

CAIUS *College*: [keez], the same as *keys*. NOT the Latin pronunciation.

CALAIS: [kal-i], to rhyme with *pally*. OR [kal-ay], to rhyme with *ballet*.

CALENDS: [kayl-endz], nearly rhyming with *tail-ends*. But those with even the rudiments of a classical education naturally prefer [kal-endz], nearly rhyming with *Lallans*.

CALIBRE. The pronunciation with the accent on the first syllable is to be preferred, and [kal-i-bə] is better than [kal-ee-bə]. But [kəl-εε-bə], accent on second syllable, is often heard.

CALLAGHAN, Irish surname: [kal-ə-hən], with H. NOT [kal-ə-gən], with G.

CALNE, Wiltshire: [kahn], to rhyme with *barn*.

56

CAMBRAI, France, known from the 1914–18 War: [kam-br__ay__]. NOT the French pronunciation.

CAMEMBERT. Pronounced in the French way.

CANA, Bible: [k__ay__n-ə], to rhyme with *gainer*. NOT [k__ah__n-ə], rhyming with *garner*.

CANBERRA: [k__a__n-bə-rə], accent on first syllable. NOT [kan-b__e__r-ə], accent on second.

CANINE: [kən-__ɛ__in], accent on second syllable. OR [k__ay__n-ɛin], accent on the first, which is the same as *cane*. NOT [k__a__n-ɛin], accent on first syllable, which is the same as *can*.

CANTON. As the name of the Chinese town, [kan-t__o__n], accent on second syllable. As a Swiss 'county', [k__a__n-ton], accent on the first.

CAPERCAILZIE: [kap-ə-k__ay__-li], no Z—which is here a Middle Scots spelling for the letter called *yogh*, which was pronounced as Y.

CAPITALIST: [k__a__p-it-ə-list], accent on first syllable. NOT [kə-p__i__t-ə-list], accent on second.

CAPOT, all the tricks in the game of Piquet: [kə-p__o__t], with T, accent on the second syllable. NOT as French.

CAPRI, Island: [k__a__p-ri], accent on first syllable. But [kap-r__ee__], accent on second, in the popular song.

CARACAS, Venezuela: [kə-r__a__k-əs], accent on second syllable. NOT [k__a__r-ə-kas], accent on first.

CARADOC, Welsh Christian name: [kə-r__a__d-ok], accent on second syllable. NOT [k__a__r-ə-dok], accent on first.

CARIBBEAN: [kar-i-bee-yən], accent on third syllable. NOT [kə-rib-i-yən], accent on second.

CARICATURE: [kar-ik-ə-tyaw], accent on last syllable; [kər-ik-ə-tyaw], accent on second syllable, has certainly been used.

CARMARTHEN, Wales: [kə-mah-dhən], accent on second syllable.

CARMICHAEL, surname: [kah-mɛik-əl], accent on second syllable. NOT [kah-mɛik-əl], accent on first.

CARNEGIE, Scotch surname: [kah-nɛg-i], second syllable to rhyme with *leg*. OR [kah-neeg-i], second syllable to rhyme with *league*.

CAROLINE, Christian name: [ka-rə-lɛin], last syllable the same as *line*. Sometimes [ka-rə-leen], last syllable the same as *lean*; occasionally [ka-rə-lin], last syllable to rhyme with *pin*.

CARPATHIAN *Mountains*: [kah-payth-yən], second syllable to rhyme with *faith*; but [kah-paydh-yən], second syllable to rhyme with *bathe*, is also used.

CASK: [kahsk]. NOT [kask].

CAST: [kahst]. NOT [kast].

CASTELNAU, London: [kahs-əl-naw], the first and third syllables being equally stressed.

CASTLE: [kahs-əl], first syllable to rhyme with *farce*. NOT [kas-əl], first syllable rhyming with *gas*.

CASUAL: [kazh-əl], two syllables. OR [kaz-yu-wəl], three.

CASUALTY: [kazh-əl-ti], three syllables. OR [kaz-yu-wəl-ti], four.

CATCH: [kach], to rhyme with *match*. OR [kech], to rhyme with *fetch*.

CATERHAM, Surrey: [kayt-ə-rəm], first syllable the same as *Kate*. NOT [kat-ə-rəm], rhyming with *scatter 'em* (i.e. *scatter them*).

CATHOLIC. The normal pronunciation is [kath-lik], first syllable to rhyme with *hath*. The old U-Catholics said [kahth-lik], first syllable to rhyme with *hearth*, and this pronunciation is now used by most keen Catholics.

CATTELL, surname. Usually [kə-tel], accent on second syllable.

CAUSEWAY: [kawz-way], as spelt. In the North of England the word is used to mean 'pavement' and is pronounced [kawz-i], to rhyme with *gauzy*; hence it is often written *causey*.

CAUSTIC. Of a remark: [kaws-tik], first syllable to rhyme with *force*. Of potash (KOH): [kos-tik], first syllable to rhyme with *Ross*.

CAVAN, Ireland: [kav-ən], the same as *cavern*. NOT [kə-van], accent on second syllable.

CAVELL, surname: [kə-vel], accent on second syllable.

CAVERNOUS: [kav-ə-nəs], accent on first syllable. OR [kəv-ur-nəs], accent on second.

CAVIAR: [kav-i-yah], three syllables. OR [kav-yah], two.

CAYENNE pepper: [kay-yen], accent on second syllable. OR [kay-yen], accent on the first. NOT [kei-yən], first syllable rhyming with *buy*.

CAYMAN, kind of crocodile: [kay-man], accent on first syllable. But the Islands of that name are, at least in the West Indies, called [kay-man], accent on second syllable.

CECIL, Christian name and surname. Usually [ses-əl], to rhyme with *nestle*. But many bearers of the surname pronounce it [sis-əl], to rhyme with *whistle*.

CEDRIC, Christian name: [seed-rik], first syllable the same as *seed*. OR [sed-rik], first syllable the same as *said*.

CELANDINE: [sel-ən-deen], last syllable the same as *dean*. OR [sel-ən-dɛin], last syllable the same as *dine*.

CELEBES *Islands*: [sel-ee-beez], accent on second syllable. NOT [sel-i-beez], accent on first.

CELTIC. There are two pronunciations, [sel-tik] with initial [s], and [kel-tik] with initial [k]. When applied to the peoples and their languages, the [s]-pronunciation used to be favoured, perhaps because of French *celtique*, but now [k] is almost universal—perhaps because of Celtic forms such as Welsh *Celtiaid*, meaning 'the Celts', in which the C is pronounced [k]. But the Scotch football club is still pronounced with [s]. Similarly CELT.

CENOTAPH: [sen-o-tahf], last syllable to rhyme with *scarf*. OR [sen-o-taf], last syllable to rhyme with *gaff*.

CENTENARY: [sen-teen-ə-ri], second syllable to rhyme with *been*. NOT [sen-ten-ə-ri], second syllable rhyming with *Ben*.

CENTRIFUGAL: [sen-trif-ʋ-gəl], accent on second syllable. NOT [sen-tri-fyoo-gəl], accent on third syllable.

CHAFF: [chahf], to rhyme with *scarf*. NOT [chaf], rhyming with *gaff*.

60

CHAFFINCH: [chahf-inch], first syllable to rhyme with *scarf*. OR [chaf-inch], first syllable to rhyme with *gaff*.

CHAGRIN: [shəg-reen], the same as *shagreen*. NOT [shag-rin], accent on first syllable.

CHANCE: [chahns], to rhyme with *France*. NOT [chans], rhyming with *manse*.

CHANDLER, surname: [chahnd-lə], first syllable to rhyme with *darned*. NOT [chand-lə], first syllable rhyming with *band*.

CHAPEL EN LE FRITH, Derbyshire. Pronounced as English, not French, that is with *en le* as [en lə].

CHARING, Kent: [cha-ring]; or [chęə-ring], rhyming with *bearing*. NOT [chah-ring], rhyming with *barring*. So also *Charing Cross*.

CHARIS, Christian name: [kar-is], to rhyme with *Harris*. NOT [char-is].

CHASSIS: [shas-i], to rhyme with *gassy*. NOT [shas-is]—or [shas-iz], rhyming with *gases*—with final consonant pronounced.

CHASTISEMENT: [chas-tęiz-mənt], accent on second syllable. [chas-tiz-mənt], accent on first syllable, is now not much used.

CHAUFFEUR: [shoh-fə], to rhyme with *sofa*. But when the word first came in, it was pronounced by the U in the French way. The pronunciation [shʌv-ə], to rhyme with *cover*, originally a U-joke, was perhaps an imitation of the way the nouveaux riches attempted the French pronunciation.

CHEMIST: [kem-ist]. The pronunciation [kim-ist], first syllable to rhyme with *rim*, is long dead, but some pharmacists use the spelling *Chymists* to show that they are old-established.

CHERTSEY, Surrey: [chu̱rt-si], to rhyme with *curtsy*. NOT [cha̱ht-si], first syllable the same as *chart*.

CHERWELL, river at Oxford: [cha̱h-wəl], first syllable to rhyme with *car*. NOT [chu̱r-wəl], first syllable rhyming with *cur*.

CHEVIOT *Hills*: [che̱ev-yət], first syllable to rhyme with *reeve*. OR [che̱v-yət], first syllable to rhyme with *rev*.

CHEYENNE, American Indians: [shɛi-ya̱n], accent on second syllable; first syllable the same as *shy*, second the same as *Anne*.

CHEYNE *Walk*, London: [cha̱y-ni], to rhyme with *brainy*.

CHICAGO: [chi-ka̱h-goh], second syllable the same as *car*. The Chicagoans call it [shi-ka̱w-goh], second syllable the same as *caw*, other Americans [shi-ka̱h-goh]. American thus has initial [sh] against English [ch].

CHICANE, in earlier Bridge: [chik-a̱yn], first syllable the same as *chick*. NOT [shik-a̱yn], first syllable the same as *chic*. Accent on second syllable. The pronunciation [chi̱k-in], the same as *chicken*, was a joke.

CHIROPODIST: [chi-ro̱p-ə-dist]. The pronunciation [kɛi-ro̱p-ə-dist], first syllable to rhyme with *buy*, seems to be dying out.

CHISHOLM, surname: [chi̱z-əm], first syllable to rhyme with *fizz* and no H in second syllable.

CHOIR: [kwah], to rhyme with *car*. OR [kwɛiə], to rhyme with *higher*. The pronunciation [koiə], the same as *coir*, often heard in Wales, is dialectal.

CHOLMONDELEY, surname: [chʌm-li], two syllables, to rhyme with *comely*. NOT as spelt.

CHRISTOPHERSON, surname: [kris-tof-ə-sən], accent on second syllable. NOT [kris-təf-ə-sən], accent on first.

CICELY, Christian name: [seis-li], to rhyme with *nicely*. OR [sis-ə-li], the same as *Sicily*.

CINCINNATI: [sin-sin-ayt-i], third syllable the same as *eight*. But the American pronunciation is [sin-sin-at-ee], third syllable the same as *at*.

CINEMA: [sin-ə-mə], first syllable the same as *sin*. The pronunciations [kin-ə-mə], first syllable the same as *kin*, and [kɛin-ee-mə], accent on the second syllable, first syllable the same as *kine*, were used in the early days, but are now dead.

CINZANO. Pronounced in the Italian way. OR in the French way. NOT [sin-zah-noh], first syllable the same as *sin*, second the same as *Czar*—the first two syllables being equally stressed.

CIRCUMSTANCES: [sur-kəm-stən-siz]. NOT [sur-kəm-stahn-siz], third syllable rhyming with *barn*.

CIRCUMSTANTIAL: [sə-kəm-stan-shəl], third syllable to rhyme with *Dan*. OR [sə-kəm-stahn-shəl], third syllable to rhyme with *darn*.

CIRENCESTER: [sis-i-tə]; or [sis-is-tə], three syllables. But the inhabitants almost all call it [sei-rən-ses-tə], four syllables, which they abbreviate to *Ciren*, pronounced [sei-rən], the same as they pronounce *siren*.

CLANCY, Irish surname: [klan-si], first syllable to rhyme with *ban*. NOT [klahn-si], first syllable rhyming with *barn*.

CLASP: [klahsp]. NOT [klasp].

63

CLASS: [klahs], to rhyme with *farce*. NOT [klas], rhyming with *gas*. Those who pronounce *class* as [klahs] think that *classy* is a non-U word, and as a joke, they pronounce it [klas̱-i], rhyming with *gassy*.

CLEF, Music: [klef], to rhyme with *deaf*. I have not been able to find out the status of the pronunciation [klaf], to rhyme with *gaff*, which does, however, exist.

CLEMATIS: [klem̱-ə-tis], accent on first syllable. NOT [kləm-ayt-is], accent on second.

CLERK: [klahk], to rhyme with *dark*. NOT [klurk], rhyming with *dirk*.

CLICHÉ: [klee̱-shay], accent on first syllable. NOT [klee-shay̱], accent on second. Foreigners use the word in the second pronunciation and with a meaning nearer its original one, which was 'the French name for a stereotype block'. 'Why didn't you publish the article I sent you?', I said to the editor of a Uruguayan philological journal. 'It was the enormous clichés,' he replied. But he was referring to some oversize diagrams.

CLIENTELE. Pronounced more or less in the French way (*clientèle*).

CLIQUE: [kleek], to rhyme with *seek*. NOT [klik], rhyming with *sick*. Similarly CLIQUEY, CLIQUISH.

CLODAGH, Irish Christian name: [kloẖ-də], to rhyme with *soda*. NOT [kloḏ-ə], rhyming with *fodder*.

CLOTH: [klawth], to rhyme with *forth*. OR [kloth], to rhyme with *moth*.

CLOUGH, surname: [klʌf], to rhyme with *stuff*.

64

CLOVELLY, Devon: [klə-vẹl-i], accent on second syllable.

CLUNIES, Scotch surname: [klọọn-iz], to rhyme with *loonies*.

COBALT: [kọh-bawlt], accent on first syllable. OR [kə-bawlt] accent on the second. The latter pronunciation is used more by those interested in Art than by those interested in Chemistry.

COBRA: [kọhb-rə], first syllable to rhyme with *lobe*. NOT [kọb-rə], first syllable rhyming with *lob*.

COCKBURN, surname: [kọh-bən], to rhyme with *Holborn*.

CODICIL: [kọhd-i-sil],ˋ first syllable the same as *code*. OR [kọd-i-sil], first syllable the same as *cod*.

COFFEE: [kọf-i], to rhyme with *toffee*; the pronunciation [kawf-i], first syllable to rhyme with *wharf*, which, at one time, was U, is to-day only American.

COGHLAN, Irish surname: [kọk-lən], first syllable the same as *cock*. NOT [kọg-lən], first syllable the same as *cog*.

COGNISANT: [kọg-niz-ənt], accent on first syllable. NOT [kog-nẹiz-ənt], accent on second.

COKE, surname: usually [kʊk], the same as *cook*. NOT [kohk], the same as *coke*.

COLBURN, surname: [kọh-bən], to rhyme with *Holborn*. NOT as spelt.

COLCHESTER: [kọhl-ches-tə], first syllable the same as *coal*. NOT [kọl-ches-tə], first syllable the same as *col*.

COLCLOUGH, surname: [kọl-clʌf], second syllable to rhyme with *stuff*, first with *doll*.

COLERAINE, Ireland: [kọhl-rayn], two syllables, equally stressed. NOT [kol-ə-rayn], three syllables, accent on last.

COLMAN, surname, well known as that of a mustard-maker: [kọl-mən], first syllable to rhyme with *doll*. NOT [kọhl-mən], first syllable rhyming with *dole*—this last pronunciation is, however, almost universal in application to the Mustard itself.

COLNEY *Hatch*: [kọh-ni], to rhyme with *bony*. NOT [kọl-ni], as spelt.

COLOGNE: [kə-lọhn], to rhyme with *alone*.

COLOMBIA: [kə-lʌm-byə], second syllable to rhyme with *come*; [kə-lọm-byə], second syllable to rhyme with *Tom*, is also used.

COLOMBO: [kə-lʌm-boh], second syllable to rhyme with *come*. NOT [kə-lọm-boh], second syllable rhyming with *Tom*.

COLONSAY, Scotland: [kọl-ọn-say], the three syllables being equally stressed.

COLOPHON, of a book: [kọhl-ə-fon], first syllable the same as *coal*. OR [kọl-ə-fon], first syllable to rhyme with *doll*.

COLQUHOUN, Scotch surname: [kə-họọn].

COMBAT: [kʌm-bat], first syllable the same as *come*; but [kọm-bat], first syllable to rhyme with *Tom*, is often used.

COMBERMERE, peer's title: [kʌm-bə-meeə], first two syllables to rhyme with *number*. NOT [kọọm-bə-meeə], first syllable rhyming with *doom*, or [kʊm-bə-meeə], first syllable rhyming with *room*, or [kọhm-bə-meeə], first syllable the same as *comb*.

COMMAND: [kə-mahnd], second syllable to rhyme with *darned*. NOT [kə-mand], second syllable rhyming with *tanned*.

COMMANDANT: [kom-ən-dant], accent on last syllable, which rhymes with *cant*. NOT [kom-ən-da̱ẖnt], last syllable rhyming with *can't*.

COMMENT, verb and noun: [ko̱m-ent], accent on first syllable. NOT [kə-ment], accent on second.

COMPARABLE: [ko̱m-prə-bəl], three syllables, accent on first. NOT [kom-pe̱ə̱-rə-bəl], four syllables, accent on second.

COMPROMISE: [ko̱m-prə-mɛiz], accent on first syllable, last syllable to rhyme with *rise*. NOT [kəm-pro̱m-is], accent on second syllable, last part the same as *promise*.

COMRADE: [ko̱m-rid], first syllable to rhyme with *Tom*, is to-day much more usual than [kʌm-rid], first syllable the same as *come*.

CONAN, surname (well known in *Conan Doyle*): [ko̱ẖn-ən], first syllable the same as *cone*. NOT [ko̱n-ən], first syllable the same as *con*.

CONCERTO: [kon-che̱ə̱-toh], second syllable the same as *chair*. NOT [kon-su̱ṟ-toh], second syllable the same as *sir*.

CONDOLENCE: [kon-do̱ẖl-əns], accent on second syllable. NOT [ko̱n-dəl-əns], accent on first.

CONDUIT *Street*, London: [kʌn-dit], two syllables, to rhyme with *pundit*. NOT [ko̱n-dyʊ-wit], three syllables. Many U-people feel to-day that their correct pronunciation is too bizarre and use a compromise such as [ko̱n-dit].

CONFESSOR: [kən-fe̱s-ə], accent on second syllable; [ko̱n-fes-ə], accent on first, is a U-Catholic pronunciation.

CONGERIES: [ko̱n-jə-reez], three syllables, accent on the first. OR [kon-je̱-ri-eez], four syllables, accent on the second.

CONGRESBURY, Somerset: [koͦonz-ber-i], three syllables, first to rhyme with *moons*. NOT as spelt.

CONJUGAL: [koͦn-jʊ-gəl], accent on first syllable. NOT [kon-joͦoͦ-gəl], accent on second.

CONJURE. Two different verbs, pronounced differently: [kʌn-jə], to rhyme with *sponger*, to do conjuring tricks; and [kən-ja͟w], accent on second syllable, meaning 'to swear by'.

CONSIDINE, surname: [koͦn-si-dɛin], last syllable the same as *dine*. Sometimes [koͦn-si-din], last syllable the same as *din*.

CONSOMMÉ: pronounced more or less in the French way. The slang expression *in the consommé*, meaning 'in the soup' is old-fashioned, perhaps no longer used; in it, *consommé* was pronounced [kon-soͦm-i], accent on second syllable, last two syllables to rhyme with *Tommy*.

CONSTABLE: [kʌns-tə-bəl], to rhyme with *Dunstable*. NOT [koͦn-stəb-el] first syllable rhyming with *don*.

CONSTRUE: as verb, [kəns-troͦoͦ], accent on second syllable; as noun, [koͦns-troo], accent on first.

CONSUMMATE, verb: [koͦn-sʊ-mayt], accent on first syllable. Adjective: [kən-sʌm-it], accent on second.

CONTEMPLATIVE: [kən-tem-plə-tiv], accent on second syllable, sometimes [koͦn-təm-play-tiv], accent on first. NOT [kon-təm-play-tiv], accent on third.

CONTRALTO: [kon-tral-toh], second syllable to rhyme with *pal*. NOT [kon-tra͟hl-toh], second syllable rhyming with *Carl*; or [kon-tra͟wl-toh], second syllable rhyming with *Paul*.

CONTROVERSY: [kən-troͦv-ə-si], accent on second syllable. OR [koͦn-trə-vur-si], accent on first.

CONTUMELY: [kon-tyọọ-mə-li], accent on second syllable. NOT [kọn-tyʊ-mə-li], accent on first.

CONYBEARE, surname. The first two syllables can be pronounced in three ways—to rhyme with *bunny*, *bonny*, or *bony*, respectively; the last syllable can be pronounced in two ways— the same as *bear* or the same as *beer*. There are thus $3 \times 2 = 6$ possible pronunciations: [kʌn-i-bɛə], [kọn-i-bɛə], [kọhn-i-bɛə] [kʌn-i-beeə], [kọn-i-beeə], [kọhn-i-beeə]. Perhaps the first— first two syllables to rhyme with *bunny*, last the same as *bear*— is to be preferred.

CONYNGHAM, surname: [kʌn-ing-əm], the same as *Cunningham*. NOT [kọn-ing-əm], first syllable the same as *con*.

COPENHAGEN: [koh-pen-hạy-gən], last two syllables to rhyme with *pagan*. NOT [koh-pen-hạh-gən], third syllable rhyming with *par*, which is American.

COQUETTE: [kok-ẹt], first syllable the same as *cock*. NOT [kohk-ẹt], first syllable the same as *coke*.

CORDOBA: [kaw-dọh-və], accent on second syllable, last two syllables the same as *Dover*. OR [kạw-do-və], accent on first syllable. (B pronounced [v].)

CORONARY: [kọr-ən-ri], three syllables, accent on the first. NOT [kə-rọhn-ə-ri], four syllables, accent on the second.

CORSTORPHINE, Scotland: [kos-tạw-fin], accent on second syllable. NOT [kạw-stə-fɛin], accent on first.

COST: [kawst], to rhyme with *forced*. OR [kost], to rhyme with *bossed*. Similarly, COSTLY: [kạwst-li], not [kọst-li].

COSTAIN, surname: [kọs-tayn], accent on first syllable. NOT [kə-stạyn], accent on second.

69

COUGH: [kawf], to rhyme with *wharf*. OR [kof], to rhyme with *doff*.

COULSON, surname: [kọọl-sən], first syllable the same as *cool*. OR [kọhl-sən], first syllable the same as *coal*.

COUP: [koo], no P, the same as *coo*. NOT [koop], with P, the same as *coop*.

COUPON: [kọọp-on], first syllable to rhyme with *troop*. NOT [kyọọp-on], first syllable rhyming with *dupe*; or [kọọp-ong], or [kyọọp-ong], second syllable to rhyme with *long*.

COURTENAY, surname: [kạwt-ni], two syllables, first the same as *caught*.

COURTEOUS: [kụṛt-yəs], first syllable the same as *curt*. OR [kạwt-yəs], first syllable the same as *caught*. Similarly DISCOURTEOUS.

COUTTS, surname: [koots], to rhyme with *hoots*.

COVENT *Garden*: [kʌv-ənt], first syllable to rhyme with *dove*. NOT [kọv-ənt], first syllable rhyming with *of*.

COVENTRY: [kʌv-ən-tri], first syllable to rhyme with *glove*, is the better pronunciation; but [kọv-ən-tri], first syllable to rhyme with *of*, is more widely used to-day.

COVERLEY, surname. Well known from *Sir Roger de Coverley*, kind of dance: [kʌv-ə-li], first syllable to rhyme with *love*. NOT [kọv-ə-li], first syllable rhyming with *of*.

COWPER, surname. Usually [kọọp-ə], first syllable the same as *coop*. But sometimes [kọụ-pə], first syllable the same as *cow*. Despite considerable discussion it is not certain which of the two pronunciations the poet used for his name.

CRAFTY: [kra̱hf-ti], first syllable to rhyme with *scarf*. NOT [kra̱f-ti], first syllable rhyming with *gaff*.

CRAWSHAW, surname: [kra̱sh-aw], first syllable the same as *crash*. But many bearers of the name pronounce it [kra̱w-shaw], as spelt.

CREDENCE: [kre̱ed-əns], first syllable to rhyme with *bead*. NOT [kre̱d-əns], first syllable rhyming with *bed*.

CREIGHTON, surname: [kre̱it-ən], to rhyme with *Brighton*.

CRESCENT: [kre̱s-ənt], first syllable to rhyme with *bless*. NOT [kre̱z-ənt], first syllable rhyming with *fez*.

CRICHTON, surname: [kre̱it-ən], to rhyme with *Brighton*.

CRIEFF, Scotland: [kreef], to rhyme with *grief*. NOT [kre̱e-yef], two syllables, rhyming with *Kiev*.

CRITCHLEY, surname: [kri̱ch-li], to rhyme with *richly*. NOT [kre̱ich-li], rhyming with *Pytchley*.

CROCHET: [kro̱h-shi], no T. In the verb, too, the T is silent; for instance *she was crocheting*: [kro̱h-shi-ing]; not [kro̱h-shə-ting], with T.

CROMARTY, Scotland: [kro̱m-ə-ti], first syllable to rhyme with *Tom*. NOT [krʌm-ə-ti], first syllable the same as *crumb*.

CROMWELL, surname, particularly of *Oliver Cromwell*: [kro̱m-wəl], first syllable to rhyme with *Tom*. But formerly—and still in Ireland: [krʌm-wəl], first syllable the same as *crumb*.

CROQUET: [kro̱h-ki], to rhyme with *poky*. NOT [kro̱h-kay], second syllable rhyming with *pay*. No T.

71

CROSS: [kraws], to rhyme with *horse*. OR [kros], to rhyme with *Ross*.

CRUEL: [krool], one syllable, to rhyme with *stool*. OR [kroo-əl].

CRUIKSHANK, surname: [kruk-shank], first syllable the same as *crook*.

CRUX: [krʌks], to rhyme with *ducks*. Since many people who deal with textual cruces—these are pronounced [kroo-seez]—have had a classical education, it is natural that the pronunciation [kruks], the same as *crooks*, is sometimes heard.

CUCUMBER: [kyoo-kʌm-bə]. The pronunciation [kou-kʌm-bə], first syllable the same as *cow*, was known as old-fashioned U about 1900. It does not exist, even as a joke, to-day.

The CUILLINS, Scotland: [kool-inz].

CUL-DE-SAC: [kul-də-sak], first syllable to rhyme with *bull*. NOT the French pronunciation; or, [kʌl-də-sak], first syllable rhyming with *dull*.

CULINARY: [kʌl-in-ri], three syllables, first the same as *cull*. [kyool-in-ə-ri], four syllables, first to rhyme with *pool*, is old-fashioned.

CULLODEN, battle: [kə-lohd-ən], second syllable the same as *load*. NOT [kə-lod-ən], last part rhyming with *Flodden*; or [kə-lʌd-ən], last part rhyming with *sudden*.

CULT: [kʌlt]. OR, the French pronunciation (of *culte*).

CUNEIFORM: [kyoo-nay-i-fawm], four syllables, accent on the second, which is the same as *neigh*. [kyoo-ni-fawm], to rhyme with *uniform*, is also used.

72

CURAÇAO, island (and liqueur): [kyaw-rə-soh], first syllable to rhyme with *jaw*, accent on last syllable, which rhymes with *Joe*.

CURATOR: [kyaw-rayt-ə], first syllable the same as *cure*. NOT [kyoo-rayt-ə], first syllable the same as *queue*.

The CURRAGH, Ireland: [kʌr-ə], to rhyme with *borough*.

CUSACK, surname. Usually [kyooz-ak], first syllable to rhyme with *dues*. NOT [kʌz-ak], first syllable to rhyme with *buzz*.

CUZCO (or CUSCO), Peru: [kʌz-koh], first syllable to rhyme with *buzz*.

CYNOSURE: [sin-o-zhə], last syllable the same as second syllable of *azure*; or [sin-o-shə], last syllable the same as that of most people's pronunciation of *Persia*; accent on first syllable. NOT [sɛin-oh-zhə] or [sɛin-oh-shə], accent on second.

CYRENAICA: [sɛi-rə-nay-i-kə], five syllables.

CZECHO-SLOVAKIA: [chek-oh sləv-ahk-yə], fourth syllable to rhyme with *bark*, or [chek-oh sləv-ak-yə], fourth syllable to rhyme with *back*. Czechs, trying to be more English than the English, usually say [chek-oh sləv-ayk-yə], fourth syllable to rhyme with *bake*, when speaking English.

DAFT. The word has come in from Northern Dialect, in which it is very often pronounced [daft], to rhyme with *gaffed*. Many educated speakers feel the combination [aft] to be wrong— for, in many words, they have [ahft] for this, e.g. *after* as [ahf-tə], to rhyme with *laughter*, not [aft-tə]. If they use the word *daft*, such speakers therefore pronounce it [dahft], to rhyme with *laughed*.

73

DAHOMEY: [dah-həm-i], accent on first syllable. OR [dah-hoh-mi], accent on second.

DAIS: [days], the same as *dace*. [day-is], two syllables, is pedantic.

DALGLEISH, Scotch surname: [dal-gleesh], accent on second syllable, which rhymes with *leash*.

DALKEITH, Scotland: [dal-keeth], accent on second syllable, first syllable to rhyme with *pal*. NOT [dawl-keeth], accent on first syllable, which rhymes with *Paul*.

DAMASCUS: [də-mas-kəs], second syllable to rhyme with *gas*. OR [də-mahs-kəs], second syllable to rhyme with *farce*.

DAMIAN, Christian name: [daym-yən], first syllable the same as *dame*.

DANCE: [dahns], to rhyme with *France*. NOT [dans], rhyming with *manse*.

DANZIG: [dant-sig]. NOT [dan-zig].

DATA: [day-tə], to rhyme with *cater*. NOT [dah-tə], rhyming with *carter*; or [da-tə], rhyming with *scatter*.

DAVENTRY, Northamptonshire: [dav-ən-tri], three syllables. The old pronunciation [dayn-tri], to rhyme with *Aintree*, was essentially killed in the nineteen-thirties, because the B.B.C. had a transmitter there, and they pronounced the name [dav-ən-tri], as spelt.

DAVIES, Welsh surname: [day-vis], to rhyme with *Mavis*. NOT [day-veez], second syllable rhyming with *squeeze*.

DEATH, surname: usually [deeth], to rhyme with *wreath*. NOT [deth], the same as *death*.

74

DEAUVILLE, France: [dọh-vil]. The French pronunciation would be affected.

DEBORAH, Christian name: [dẹb-ə-rə], accent on first syllable. It is a Hebrew name and English Jews call it [də-bạw-rə], accent on second syllable.

DECIES, peer's title: [dẹe-sees].

DECOROUS: [dẹk-ə-rəs], accent on first syllable; better than [də-kạw-rəs], accent on second. But DECORUM is pronounced with this accentuation: [də-kạw-rəm].

DE CRESPIGNY, surname: [də-krẹp-i-ni], no S, accent on second syllable.

DEFECT: [də-fẹkt], to rhyme with *effect*; better than [dẹe-fekt], accent on first syllable.

DEFICIT: [dẹf-is-it], first syllable the same as *deaf*. OR [dẹef-is-it], first syllable to rhyme with *reef*.

DEIFY: [dẹe-i-fɛi], first syllable to rhyme with *bee*. NOT [dạy-i-fɛi], first syllable rhyming with *bay*.

DEIGHTON, surname: [dạy-tən], to rhyme with *Satan*. NOT [dẹit-ən], rhyming with *Brighton*.

DEIRDRE, Irish Christian name: [dẹeə-dri].

DE LA MARE, surname: [dẹl-ə-mah], accent on first syllable, last the same as *ma*. NOT [dẹl-ə-mɛə] or [del-ə-mẹə], last syllable as spelt.

DE LA WARR, peer's title: [dẹl-ə-wẹə], the first and third syllables being equally stressed. The pronunciation sounds very like the English pronunciation of U.S. *Delaware*.

DEMAND: [də-mahnd], second syllable to rhyme with *darned*. NOT [də-mand], second syllable rhyming with *band*.

DEMERARA (sugar): [dem-ə-rɛ̱ə-rə], third syllable to rhyme with *pair*. OR [dem-ə-rah-rə], third syllable to rhyme with *par*.

DENIGRATE: [dɛn-ig-rayt], accent on first syllable, which is the same as *den*. NOT [dɛ̱ɛn-ig-rayt], first syllable the same as *dean*; or [dee-nɛ̱ig-rayt], accent on second syllable.

DEPOT: [dɛp-oh], first syllable to rhyme with *pep*. [dɛ̱ɛp-oh], first syllable to rhyme with *peep*, is now American; its main meaning is 'railway-station'. No T.

DERBY: [dah-bi], first syllable to rhyme with *car*. NOT [du̱r-bi], first syllable rhyming with *cur*.

DE RESZKE, surname: [də-rɛs-ki], three syllables. When this was used for a brand of cigarettes the purchasers mostly pronounced the name [də-rɛsk], two syllables.

DE SAUMAREZ, peer's title: [də-sʌm-ər-iz], last part the same as *summaries*.

DESPICABLE: [dɛs-pik-ə-bəl], accent on first syllable. NOT [des-pi̱k-ə-bəl], accent on second.

DETONATE: [dɛt-ə-nayt], first syllable to rhyme with *bet*. OR [dɛ̱ɛt-ə-nayt], first syllable to rhyme with *beat*.

DETOUR: [dɛ̱ɛ-taw], accent on first syllable, is now more usual than the older [də-to̱ọə], or [də-ta̱w], accent on second syllable.

DEVOLVE: [də-vo̱lv]. NOT [də-vo̱hlv].

DIABETIC: [dɛiə-bɛt-ik], second syllable the same as *bet*, is more usual than [dɛiə-bɛ̱ɛt-ik], second syllable the same as *beat*.

76

DIAMOND: [da͟h-mənd], first syllable to rhyme with *par*. OR [dɛi͟ə-mənd], first part to rhyme with *higher*.

DIDN'T IT?: [di͟d-ənt i͟t]. NOT [di͟d-ə-nit], no middle T. Children often say *I didn't!* with [di͟t-ənt], first syllable to rhyme with *bit*.

DIFFERENT: [di͟f-rənt], two syllables. OR [di͟f-ə-rənt], three syllables.

DIGRESS: [dig-re͟s], first syllable the same as *dig*. OR [dɛig-re͟s], first syllable to rhyme with that of *tiger*.

DILATE: [dɛil-a͟yt], first syllable to rhyme with *pile*. NOT [dil-a͟yt], first syllable rhyming with *pill*.

DILATORY: [di͟l-ə-tri], three syllables, accent on first. NOT [dɛi-la͟yt-ə-ri], four syllables, accent on second.

DILEMMA: [dil-e͟m-ə], first syllable to rhyme with *pill*. OR [dɛil-e͟m-ə], first syllable to rhyme with *pile*.

DINGHY: [di͟ng-i], to rhyme with *stringy* is the Naval pronunciation; but [di͟ng-gi] is often used.

DIOCESAN: [dɛi-o͟s-əz-ən], accent on second syllable. NOT [dɛi-o-se͟ez-ən], accent on third.

DIPHTHERIA: [dif-the͟eə-ri-yə], first syllable to rhyme with *sniff*. But the pronunciation [dip-the͟eə-ri-yə], first syllable the same as *dip*, is often used.

DIPHTHONG: [di͟f-thong], first syllable to rhyme with *sniff*. NOT [di͟p-thong], first syllable rhyming with *snip*.

DIRECT: [di-re͟kt]. OR [dɛi-re͟kt].

77

DISAGREEABLE: [dis-ə-gri̱-yə-bəl], five syllables; but often pronounced [dis-ə-gri̱b-əl], four syllables, last two to rhyme with *dribble*.

DISCERN: [di-su̱rn]. OR [di-zu̱rn].

DISCIPLINARY: [di̱s-i-plin-ə-ri], accent on first syllable, third syllable to rhyme with *win*. OR [dis-i-plɛi̱n-ə-ri], accent on third syllable, which rhymes with *wine*.

DISPATCH: [dis-pa̱ch]. OR [dəs-pa̱ch].

DISPUTABLE: [dis-pyo̱ot-ə-bəl], accent on second syllable. NOT [di̱s-pyʊt-ə-bəl], accent on first.

DISSOLVE: [diz-o̱lv]. NOT [diz-o̱hlv].

DIVAN: [di-va̱n], accent on second syllable, which is the same as *van*. NOT [dɛi̱-van], accent on first. [di-va̱hn], accent on second syllable, which rhymes with *barn*, is often heard, and must be used when *The Divan*, the one-time Turkish Council of State, is meant.

DIVULGE: [div-ᴧlj], first syllable to rhyme with *spiv*. OR [dɛiv-ᴧlj], first syllable the same as *dive*.

DNIEPER, river in U.S.S.R.: [dne̱ep-ə], to rhyme with *leaper*.

DNIESTER, river in U.S.S.R.: [dne̱est-ə], to rhyme with *Easter*.

DOBELL, surname: [do-be̱l], accent on second syllable.

DOCILE: [do̱hs-ɛil], first syllable the same as *dose*, is more usual than [do̱s-ɛil], first syllable the same as *doss*.

DOCTRINAL: [dok-trɛi̱n-əl], accent on second syllable. NOT [do̱k-trin-əl], accent on first.

DOG: [dog]. The pronunciation [dawg], to rhyme with *morgue*, was apparently once U.

DOHERTY, Irish surname: [do̱-hə-ti], with Scotch *ch* in *loch* for the [h]. NOT [do̱h-hə-ti], first syllable the same as *dough*.

DOLGELLEY, Wales: [dol-ge̱th-li], second syllable to rhyme with *breath*.

DOMINICA: [də-mi̱n-ik-ə], accent on second syllable, is normal, but, in the West Indies, the island is called [dom-in-e̱ek-ə], accent on third syllable.

DOMINICAN, Republic or Friars: [də-mi̱n-ik-an], accent on second syllable.

DONAGHUE, Irish surname: [dʌn-ə-hyʊ], first syllable the same as *dun*. NOT [do̱n-ə-gyʊ], first syllable the same as *don*, last syllable the same as the second syllable of *ague*.

DONEGAL: [dʌn-i-ga̱wl], first syllable the same as *dun*. But English people often call it [don-i-ga̱wl], first syllable the same as *don*.

DONNE, surname. The poet is called [dʌn], the same as *done*. NOT [don], the same as *don*.

DONOUGHMORE, peer's title: [dʌn-o-ma̱w], accent on last syllable, first syllable the same as *dun*.

DOREEN, Christian name: [do-re̱en], accent on second syllable. NOT [da̱w-reen], accent on first.

DOUR: [dooə], the same as *doer*. NOT [do̱u-wə], rhyming with *tower*.

DOYEN. Pronounced in the French way. OR [do̱i-yen], first syllable to rhyme with *boy*.

DROGHEDA, Ireland: [dro̱i-də], to rhyme with *avoid 'er* (i.e. *avoid her*).

DROLL: [drohl], to rhyme with *bowl*. NOT [drol], rhyming with *doll*.

DROMEDARY: [dro̱m-ə-dər-i], first syllable to rhyme with *Tom*; [drʌm-ə-dər-i], first syllable the same as *drum*, is old-fashioned.

DRYSDALE, surname: [dre̱iz-dayl], first syllable the same as *dries*.

DUBIOUS: [dyo̱o̱b-yəs], first syllable to rhyme with *tube*. NOT [do̱o̱b-yəs], first syllable rhyming with *boob*.

DUGUID, Scotch surname: [do̱o̱-good], almost the same as *do good*.

DUMFRIES, Scotland: [dʌm-fre̱e̱s], second syllable to rhyme with *peace*. Accent on second syllable. NOT [dʌm-fre̱e̱z], second syllable the same as *freeze*.

DUNCOMBE, surname: [dʌn-kəm], to rhyme with *bunkum*.

DUNDAS, surname: [dʌn-da̱s], accent on second syllable.

DUNEDIN, New Zealand: [dʌn-e̱e̱d-ən], first syllable the same as *dun*. Accent on second syllable. NOT [dyoon-e̱e̱d-in], first syllable the same as *dune*.

DUNRAVEN, peer's title: [dʌn-ra̱y-vən], last part the same as *raven* (noun). NOT [dʌn-ra̱v-ən], last part rhyming with *cavern*.

DUNSANY, peer's title: [dʌn-sa̱yn-i], second syllable the same as *sane*.

DUTHIE, Scotch surname: [dooth-i], to rhyme with *toothy*. But in England the name is often pronounced [dʌth-i], first syllable to rhyme with that of *Cuthbert.*

DYNEVOR, peer's title: [dɛin-və], two syllables, first the same as *dine.* NOT [din-ə-və], three syllables, first the same as *din.*

Loch EARN: [urn], to rhyme with *burn.*

EARTHENWARE: [ur-thən-wɛə]. OR [ur-dhən-wɛə].

EASTBOURNE: [eest-bawn], second syllable the same as *born.* OR [eest-booən].

EBURY *Bridge*, London: [eeb-ə-ri], first syllable to rhyme with *glebe.*

ECCLEFECHAN, Scotland: [ek-əl-fek-ən]. NOT [ek-əl-vek-ən].

ECONOMIC: [eek-ə-nom-ik], first syllable to rhyme with *seek.* OR [ek-ə-nom-ik], first syllable to rhyme with *deck.*

EDGBASTON, Birmingham: [ej-bəs-tən], accent on first syllable. [ej-bahs-tən], accent on second syllable, which rhymes with *farce*, is the old U-pronunciation, now dying out.

EDINBURGH: [ed-in-brə], three syllables. OR [ed-in-bə-rə], four.

EDWARDIAN: [ed-wawd-yən], second syllable to rhyme with *lord.* OR [ed-wahd-yən], second syllable to rhyme with *lard.*

EGO: [eg-oh], first syllable the same as *egg.* OR [eeg-oh], first syllable to rhyme with *league.*

EGREMONT, peer's title: [eg-rə-mənt], accent on first syllable, which is the same as *egg*, last two syllables to rhyme with last

81

two of *increment*. NOT [eeg-ə-mont], first two syllables the same as *eager*, last syllable rhyming with *font*.

EIGG, Scotch island: [eg], the same as *egg*.

EIRE: pronounced [ɛə-rə], to rhyme with *fairer*, by the English.

EITHER: [ɛi-dhə], first syllable to rhyme with *buy*. NOT [ee-dhə], first syllable rhyming with *bee*.

ELAINE, Christian name: [el-ayn], accent on second syllable, first to rhyme with *hell*. NOT [eel-ayn], accent on first syllable, rhyming with *heel*.

ELASTIC: [e-las-tik], second syllable to rhyme with *gas*. OR [e-lahs-tik], second syllable to rhyme with *farce*.

ELBE, river in Germany: [elb], one syllable. To use the German pronunciation (two syllables) would be slightly affected.

ELEANOR, Christian name: [el-ə-nə], three syllables, accent on the first. NOT four syllables [el-i-yə-naw], accent on the fourth, or [el-ee-yə-naw], accent on the second.

ELOCUTION: [el-ə-kyoo-shən], first syllable to rhyme with *hell*. NOT [eel-ə-kyoo-shən], first syllable rhyming with *heel*.

ELONGATED: [eel-ong-gayt-id], first syllable to rhyme with *heel*. NOT [el-ong-gayt-id], first syllable rhyming with *hell*.

ELUCIDATE: [ə-loo-si-dayt], second syllable to rhyme with *do*. OR [ə-lyoo-si-dayt], second syllable to rhyme with *dew*.

ELUDE: [ə-lood], second syllable to rhyme with *food*. OR [ə-lyood], second syllable to rhyme with *nude*.

ELVIRA, Christian name: [el-vɛiə-rə], middle part to rhyme with *higher*. NOT usually [el-veeə-rə], second syllable rhyming with *hear*.

EMACIATED: [ə-mays-i-yayt-id], second syllable to rhyme with *race*. The pronunciation [ə-mash-i-yayt-id], second syllable to rhyme with *rash*, is old-fashioned.

EMANATE: [eem-ə-nayt], first syllable to rhyme with *beam*. OR [em-ə-nayt], first syllable to rhyme with *hem*.

EMMAUS, Bible: [em-ay-əs], accent on second syllable, which rhymes with *pay*.

ENCLAVE: [en-klayv], accent on first syllable. NOT a frenchified pronunciation.

ENID, Christian name: [een-id], first syllable to rhyme with *been*. NOT [en-id], first syllable rhyming with *Ben*, though this is the 'correct' pronunciation—the name is Welsh.

ENNUI. The French pronunciation is normal. NOT [en-wee].

ENSIGN: [en-sɛin], second syllable the same as *sine*. OR [en-sin], second syllable the same as *sin*.

ENVELOPE: [on-vel-ohp], first syllable the same as *on*. OR [en-vel-ohp], first syllable to rhyme with *ten*; the latter pronunciation is invariable in Mathematics (*the envelope of a curve*). [em-blohp], two syllables, may often be heard from young persons.

ENVIRONS: [en-vir-ənz], accent on first syllable; the pronunciation [en-vɛiə-rənz], accent on second syllable, is rather old-fashioned. The verb is, however, pronounced with this accentuation: [en-vɛiə-rən]; so also is ENVIRONMENT: [en-vɛiə-rən-mənt].

83

EPHEMERAL: [ef-ĕm-ə-rəl], second syllable to rhyme with *gem*. OR [ef-ēem-ə-rəl], second syllable to rhyme with *beam*.

EPILOGUE: [ĕp-i-log], last syllable the same as *log*. NOT [ĕp-i-lohg], last syllable rhyming with *vogue*.

EPITAPH: [ĕp-i-tahf], last syllable to rhyme with *scarf*. NOT [ĕp-i-taf], last syllable rhyming with *gaff*.

EQUATION: [ə-kwāysh-ən]; the pronunciation [ə-kwāyzh-ən] is perhaps old-fashioned.

EQUERRY: [ek-wĕr-i], accent on second syllable. NOT [ĕk-wər-i], accent on first.

EQUI- in EQUIDISTANT, EQUILATERAL, etc.: [ēek-wi], first syllable to rhyme with *beak*. OR [ĕk-wi], first syllable to rhyme with *deck*.

EQUITABLE: [ĕk-wit-ə-bəl], accent on first syllable, which rhymes with *deck*. NOT [ēek-wit-ə-bəl], first syllable rhyming with *beak*; or [ek-wɛit-ə-bəl] or [eek-wɛit-ə-bəl], accent on second syllable.

ERUDITE: [ĕ-rʊ-dɛit]. OR, old-fashioned, [ĕ-ryʊ-dɛit], accent on first syllable. NOT [e-rōo-dɛit], accent on the second.

ESHER, Surrey: [ēesh-ə], first syllable to rhyme with *leash*. NOT [ɛsh-ə], first syllable rhyming with *mesh*.

ESOTERIC: [es-o-tĕ-rik], first syllable to rhyme with *less*. OR [ees-o-tĕ-rik], first syllable to rhyme with *lease*.

ESTATE: [es-tāyt], accent on second syllable. NOT [ĕs-tayt], accent on first.

ESTHER, Christian name: [ĕs-tə], the same as *ester*. NOT [ĕs-thə], with H.

ETIQUETTE: [et-i-kĕt], accent on last syllable. NOT [ĕt-ik-et], accent on first.

EVELYN, Christian name, male and female. Usually [ĕĕv-lin], two syllables, but [ĕv-ə-lin], three syllables, is also known.

EVESHAM, Worcestershire: [ĕĕv-shəm], two syllables, first to rhyme with *leave*. The pronunciation [ĭv-i-shəm], three syllables, first to rhyme with *live*, is not often heard to-day.

EVOLUTION: [eev-ə-lọọ-shən], first syllable to rhyme with *heave*. OR [ev-ə-lọọ-shən], first syllable to rhyme with *rev*. The third syllable can also be [lyọọ], to rhyme with *dew*, instead of [lọọ], to rhyme with *do*, thus [eev-ə-lyọọ-shən] or [ev-ə-lyọọ-shən].

EXASPERATED: [əg-zahs-pə-rayt-id], second syllable to rhyme with *farce*. NOT [əg-zas-pə-rayt-id], second syllable rhyming with *gas*.

EXECRABLE: [ĕk-skrə-bəl], three syllables. OR [ĕk-sek-rə-bəl], four syllables.

EXECUTIVE: [eg-zĕk-ə-tiv]. NOT [eg-zĕk-yʊ-tiv].

EXQUISITE: [ĕks-kwiz-it], accent on first syllable. OR [eks-kwĭz-it], accent on second.

EXTOL: [eks-tohl], second syllable to rhyme with *dole*. OR [eks-tọl], second syllable to rhyme with *doll*.

EXTRAORDINARY: [əks-traw-din-ri], four syllables, second to rhyme with *war*; sometimes abbreviated to three syllables, [straw-din-ri]. The pronunciations [eks-trə-aw-din-ə-ri] or [eks-trah-aw-din-ə-ri], six syllables, are rather pedantic. [eks-trə-aw-din-ɛə-ri] or [eks-trah-aw-din-ɛə-ri] is non-U.

EYRIE: [ɛə-ri], the same as *airy*. NOT [ɛiə-ri], rhyming with *fiery*.

FAEROE *Islands*: [fɛə-roh], to rhyme with *aero-*.

FAIRCLOUGH, surname: [fɛə-klʌf], second syllable to rhyme with *stuff*.

FALCON: [fawl-kən], first syllable to rhyme with *Paul*. NOT [fal-kən], first syllable rhyming with *pal*. [faw-kən], no L, is old-fashioned U, but is still used by some who have dealings with falcons.

FALKLAND *Islands*: [fawk-lənd], first syllable to rhyme with *cork*. NOT [folk-lənd], with L.

FANATIC: [fan-ət-ik], accent on first syllable. OR [fə-nat-ik], accent on second.

FANTASIA: [fan-tayz-yə], three syllables, accent on second. NOT [fan-təz-ee-yə], four syllables, accent on third.

FANTASTIC: [fan-tas-tik], second syllable to rhyme with *gas*. NOT [fan-tahs-tik], second syllable rhyming with *farce*.

FAREHAM, Hampshire: [fɛə-rəm], first syllable to rhyme with *bear*. NOT [fah-rəm], first syllable rhyming with *bar*.

FARQUHAR, Scotch surname: [fah-kə], to rhyme with *darker*. NOT [fah-kwə].

FASTEN: [fahs-ən], first syllable the same as *farce*. NOT [fas-ən], first syllable rhyming with *gas*.

FAULT: [fawlt]. NOT [folt].

FAUX, surname. Usually pronounced [foh], the same as *foe*. But [foks], the same as *fox*, and [fawks], the same as *forks*, have also been heard. The name is essentially the same as that of *Guy Fawkes*—which is pronounced [gei-foks], accent on first syllable.

FAZACKERLEY, surname: [fə-zak-ə-li], accent on second syllable.

FEATHERSTONEHAUGH, surname: [fan-shaw], two syllables, the first the same as *fan*, the second the same as *shore*. This is a famous name in that it is so often quoted as an example of the peculiarities of English spelling. As a reaction, at least one of its bearers pronounces it in full: [fedh-ə-stohn-haw], more or less as spelt.

FECUND: [fek-ʌnd], first syllable to rhyme with *deck*. OR [feek-ʌnd], first syllable to rhyme with *beak*.

FELLOW: [fel-oh], to rhyme with *bellow*. [fel-ə], to rhyme with *cellar*, is old-fashioned U. (It was also used in the expression *young-fellah-me-lad*.) This latter pronunciation also exists to-day in the working-classes, among whom the word is very common—as in, for example, *It's a fella* meaning 'it's a male'.

FENWICK, surname: [fen-ik], no W.

FERMANAGH, Ireland: [fə-man-ə], accent on second syllable, last part the same as *manor*.

Fernando POO, island: [poh], to rhyme with *doe*. NOT [poo], rhyming with *do*.

87

FERRULE: [fe-rool], second syllable to rhyme with *cool*. OR [fe-rəl], second syllable the same as '*ll* in *There'll be* . . .

FETID: [feet-id], first syllable the same as *feet*. [fet-id], first syllable to rhyme with *bet*, is rather rare nowadays.

FETISH: [fet-ish], first syllable to rhyme with *bet*. OR [feet-ish], first syllable the same as *feet*.

FETTES, Scotland: [fet-iz], to rhyme with *Betty's*.

FIANCÉ. Pronounced in the French way. NOT [fɛi-yan-si], accent on second syllable, last part rhyming with *fancy*.

FIDELITY: [fid-el-i-ti], first syllable to rhyme with *bid*. NOT [fɛid-el-i-ti], first syllable rhyming with *bide*.

FIEND: [feend], to rhyme with *screened*. NOT [fee-yənd], two syllables.

FIENNES, surname: [fɛinz], one syllable, to rhyme with *lines*. NOT [fɛi-yen-iz], three syllables, accent on the second.

FINANCE: [fin-ans], first syllable the same as *fin*. OR [fɛin-ans], first syllable the same as *fine*. Accent on second syllable. NOT [fein-ans], accent on first syllable, which is American.

FINUCANE, Irish surname: [fin-yʊ-kayn]. NOT [fin-ʊ-kayn].

FIRE: [fah], to rhyme with *car*. OR [fɛiə], to rhyme with *higher*.

FITZ- in surnames: [fits], the same as *fits*. The accent is usually on the syllable immediately following: *Fitzgibbon* [fits-gib-ən]. But in *Fitzroy* [fits-roi], it is on *Fitz-*.

FLAHERTY, Irish surname: [fla-ə-ti]. OR [flah-ə-ti], first syllable to rhyme with *car*.

88

FLASK: [flahsk]. NOT [flask].

FLORAL: [flaw-rəl], to rhyme with *plural*. NOT [flo-rəl], rhyming with *sorrel*.

FOMALHAUT, star-name: [fohm-əl-hoht], accent on first syllable, which is the same as *foam*; last syllable to rhyme with *coat*.

FOOLSCAP: [ful-skap], first syllable the same as *full*. OR [fool-skap], first syllable the same as *fool*.

FORECASTLE: [foh-kə-səl], accent on first syllable; hence the word is often spelt *fo'castle*.

FOREHEAD: [fo-rid], to rhyme with *horrid*. NOT [faw-hed], as spelt.

FORESAIL: [faws-əl], to rhyme with *dorsal*, nautical; but [faws-ayl], as spelt, is sometimes heard.

FORMAT: [faw-mat], with T; [faw-mah], no T, is not much heard to-day.

FORMIDABLE: [fawm-id-ə-bəl], accent on first syllable. NOT [fo-mid-ə-bəl], accent on second, last three syllables rhyming with *biddable*.

FORMOSA: [faw-mohz-ə], second syllable to rhyme with *doze*. OR [faw-mohs-ə], second syllable to rhyme with *dose*.

FORSYTH, surname: [fo-seith], accent on second syllable. NOT [faw-seith], accent on first.

FORTEVIOT, Scotland: [faw-tev-yət], second syllable to rhyme with *rev*. NOT [faw-teev-yət], second syllable rhyming with *reeve*.

FORWARD: [fa̱w-wəd]; but, in Foxhunting and nautically, [fo̱r-əd], no W. The U also use this latter pronunciation of the word in expressions such as *I can't get any forrader*.

FOULGER, surname: [fu̱l-jə], first syllable the same as *full*. NOT [fʌl-jə], rhyming with *bulger*. But the pronunciation [fo̱hl-jə], to rhyme with *soldier*, is known.

FOULIS, Scotch surname: [foulz], the same as *fowls*. NOT [fo̱ul-iz] or [fo̱ol-iz], two syllables.

FOWEY, Cornwall: [foi], one syllable, to rhyme with *boy*. NOT [fo̱h-wi], rhyming with *blowy*.

FRANKFURT (*-am-Main*), Germany: [fra̱nk-furt]. To use the German pronunciation would be pedantic.

FRÄULEIN. Those who know some German pronounce it in the German way. The Second War soldiers said [fra̱w-leen], first syllable to rhyme with *raw*. Many people say [fro̱u-lεin], first syllable to rhyme with *cow*.

FRIGHTFULLY: [frεi̱t-fli], two syllables, first to rhyme with *tight*. OR [frεi̱t-fəl-i], three syllables. [fra̱ht-fli], first syllable to rhyme with *tart*, has been used by the non-U to imitate the U. It is the fact that, in the twenties, some young U-speakers did approximate to this pronunciation.

FRITILLARY, butterfly: [fri-ti̱l-ə-ri], accent on second syllable; [fri̱t-il-ə-ri], accent on first, is old-fashioned.

FRIZELL, surname: [friz-e̱l], accent on second syllable.

FROME, Somerset: [froom], to rhyme with *boom*. NOT [frohm], rhyming with *Rome*.

90

FRONTIER: [frʌn-teeə], first syllable to rhyme with *dun*. [frɒn-teeə], first syllable to rhyme with *don*, can still be heard.

FROST: [frawst], to rhyme with *forced*. OR [frost], to rhyme with *bossed*.

FROTH: [frawth], to rhyme with *forth*. OR [froth], to rhyme with *moth*.

FROUDE, surname: [frood], to rhyme with *brood*. NOT [froud], rhyming with *loud*.

FULCRUM: [fʌl-krəm], first syllable to rhyme with *dull*. NOT [fʊl-krəm], first syllable the same as *full*.

FULMINATE: [fʌl-min-ayt], first syllable to rhyme with *dull*. OR [fʊl-min-ayt], first syllable the same as *full*.

Barrow-in-FURNESS: [fur-nəs], the same as *furnace*. NOT [fur-nes], accent on second syllable.

FURORE: [fyʊ-raw-ri], three syllables, accent on second. NOT [fyoo-raw], two syllables, accent on first.

FYLDE, Lancashire: [feild], the same as *filed*.

GAELIC. Englishmen use the pronunciation [gayl-ik], first syllable the same as *gale*. The pronunciation [gahl-ik], the same as *garlic*, is often felt to be 'more correct'.

GAITSKELL, surname: [gayt-skil], second syllable the same as *skill*. NOT as spelt.

GALA: [gahl-ə], first syllable to rhyme with *marl*. OR [gayl-ə], first syllable the same as *gale*.

GALANTINE: [gal-ən-teen], last syllable to rhyme with *seen*; [gal-ən-tɛin], last syllable to rhyme with *sign*, is old-fashioned.

GALAPAGOS *Islands*: [gəl-ap-ə-gos], accent on second syllable. OR [gal-ə-payg-os], accent on third.

GALLAGHER, Irish surname: [gal-ə-hə]. NOT [gal-ə-gə].

GALLANT: [gal-ənt], accent on first syllable, in the meaning 'brave'; but [gəl-ant], accent on the second, when it is used of the behaviour of a man to a woman—the word is then felt to be deliberately old-fashioned.

GAMUT: [gam-ət], first syllable to rhyme with *ham*. NOT [gaym-ət], first syllable the same as *game*.

GARAGE: [gar-ahzh], to rhyme with *barrage*. NOT [gar-ij], rhyming with *carriage*; or [gə-rahzh], accent on second syllable.

GARETH, Christian name: [ga-rith], first syllable the same as that of *garret*. NOT [gɛə-rith], first syllable the same as that of *garish*.

GARIBALDI, the Italian patriot; also the name of an old-fashioned biscuit: [gar-i-bawl-di], accent on third syllable, which is the same as *ball*.

GARMISCH, Germany: [gah-mish].

GARRULOUS: [gar-ʊ-ləs]. OR [gar-yʊ-ləs].

GASCOIGNE, surname: [gas-koin], accent on second syllable, which rhymes with *join*. NOT [gas-koin], accent on first syllable.

92

GASEOUS: [gas-yəs], first syllable the same as *gas*. OR [gays-yəs], first syllable to rhyme with *pace*.

GASP: [gahsp]. NOT [gasp].

GASTRIC: [gas-trik], first syllable the same as *gas*. NOT [gahs-trik], first syllable rhyming with *farce*.

GATH, Bible: [gath], to rhyme with *hath*.

GAZA, Bible: [gahz-ə], first syllable to rhyme with *cars*. NOT [gayz-ə], rhyming with *razor*.

GEDDES, surname: [ged-iz], two syllables.

GENEALOGY: [jee-ni-yal-ə-ji]. NOT [jee-ni-yol-ə-ji], as if the word ended in -*ology*.

GENEVIEVE, Christian name: [jen-ə-veev], first syllable to rhyme with *hen*.

GENIUS: [jeen-yəs]. The pronunciation [jeen-i-yʌs], three syllables, accent on the last, has been used facetiously.

GENOA: [jen-oh-wə], accent on first syllable. NOT [jen-oh-ə], accent on second.

GENTLEMEN: [jen-təl-mən], last syllable the same as second syllable of *woman*. But in toasts, etc., it is pronounced [jen-təl-men], last syllable the same as *men*—thus affording the only example in English of the vocative plural being different in pronunciation from the normal plural form.

GENUINE: [jen-yʊ-win], last syllable to rhyme with *pin*. NOT [jen-yʊ-wɛin], last syllable rhyming with *pine*.

GEOGHEGAN, Irish surname: [gay-gən], to rhyme with *Dagon* (Bible).

93

GEORGINA, Christian name. Perhaps not very common to-day. When it was in full use it was often pronounced by the U as [jaw-jɛi-nə], last two syllables to rhyme with *liner*, though sometimes as [jaw-jee-nə], last two syllables to rhyme with *leaner*. *Gina* [jee-nə] is sometimes short for *Georgina*, more usually perhaps for *Regina*. But many Ginas are doubtless called after the Italian film-star *Gina Lollobrigida*.

GERAGHTY, Irish surname: [gɛr-ə-ti], accent on first syllable.

GERAINT, Christian name. Usually [jər-aynt], second syllable to rhyme with *paint*. The correct Welsh pronunciation [gər-ɛint], second syllable to rhyme with *pint*, is naturally used by those familiar with Wales.

GERONTIUS, name, well known from Elgar's *Dream of Gerontius*: [jə-ront-i-yəs]. NOT [gə-ront-i-yəs], although the latter is 'more correct', for Latin G is pronounced [g], never [j].

GERVASE, Christian name: [jur-vis], to rhyme with *service*. NOT [jə-vayz], accent on second syllable, which rhymes with *daze*.

GESTURE: [jɛs-chə], first syllable the same as *Jess*. NOT [gɛs-chə], first syllable the same as *guess*.

GET: [get], to rhyme with *pet*. OR [git], to rhyme with *pit*.

GEYSER: [gayz-ə], the same as *gazer* (one who gazes). OR [geez-ə], to rhyme with *Caesar*.

GHASTLY: [gahst-li]. NOT [gast-li], first syllable the same as *gassed*.

GHOUL: [gool], the same as *Goole*. NOT [goul], rhyming with *howl*.

94

GIAOUR (Byron): [jou̯-wə], to rhyme with *flower*.

GILLETT, surname. Often pronounced [jil-ẹt], accent on second syllable, first the same as *Jill*; but sometimes [gil̯-it], to rhyme with *billet*, first syllable the same as *gill* (fish).

GILLIAN, Christian name: [jil̯-yən], first syllable the same as *Jill*. NOT [gil̯-yən], first syllable the same as *gill* (fish).

GILLINGHAM, Kent: [jil̯-ing-əm], first syllable the same as *Jill*. But the place of the same name in Dorset is pronounced [gil̯-ing-əm], first syllable the same as *gill* (fish).

GILLOW, surname: [gil̯-oh], first syllable the same as *gill* (fish). NOT [jil̯-oh], first syllable the same as *Jill*.

GIMSON, surname: [jim̯-sən], first syllable the same as *Jim*. NOT [gim̯-sən].

GIRAFFE: [jrahf], one syllable, to rhyme with *scarf*; or [jə-rạhf], two syllables. NOT [ji-rạf], second syllable rhyming with *gaff*.

GIRL: [gurl], to rhyme with *curl*. This pronunciation is used by most speakers, whether they are U or non-U. But there are a number of other pronunciations of the word which were once used by U-speakers and some of these still survive. [gel], to rhyme with *bell*, and [gal], to rhyme with *pal*, seem really to have died out. [gɛəl], to rhyme with *there'll* (as in *there'll be snow*) still survives among the female U.

GLACIAL: [glạys-yəl], first syllable to rhyme with *pace*. OR [glạysh-əl].

GLAMIS *Castle*: [glahmz], to rhyme with *harms*. NOT [glạm-is], two syllables, first rhyming with *ham*.

95

GLANCE: [glahns], to rhyme with *France*. NOT [glans], rhyming with *manse*.

GLASS: [glahs], to rhyme with *farce*. NOT [glas], rhyming with *gas*.

GLASTONBURY, Somerset: [glas-tən-bər-i], first syllable to rhyme with *gas*. NOT [glahs-tən-bər-i], first syllable rhyming with *farce*.

GLOAG, Scotch surname: [glohg], to rhyme with *rogue*. NOT [gloh-ag], two syllables.

GNOME: [nohm], no G. The word worries the uneducated and I have heard [gə-nohm], two syllables, and also [gohm]; in this last case the speaker knew that one of the two initial consonants was silent, but made N silent instead of G.

GODALMING, Surrey: [god-əl-ming], accent on first syllable. NOT [gəd-al-ming], accent on second.

GODOLPHIN, surname: [gə-dol-fin], accent on second syllable.

GOLF: [gof], to rhyme with *scoff*, no L; or [golf], to rhyme with first part of *dolphin*. NOT [gohlf], rhyming with first part of *soulful*.

GOLIGHTLY, surname: [gə-leit-li], accent on second syllable.

GOMERSALL, surname: [gom-ə-səl], first syllable to rhyme with *Tom*. NOT [gʌm-ə-səl], first syllable the same as *gum*.

GOMME, surname: [gom], to rhyme with *Tom*. NOT [gʌm], the same as *gum*.

GONDOLA: [gon-də-lə], accent on first syllable. NOT [gon-dohl-ə], accent on second.

GONE: [gawn], to rhyme with *born*. NOT [gon], rhyming with *on*.

GOOSEBERRY: [gu̯z-bər-i]. NOT [go̯os-bər-i], first syllable the same as *goose*.

GORLESTON, Norfolk: [ga̱wl-stən], two syllables. NOT [ga̱wl-ə-stən], three.

GOTHENBURG = *Göteborg*, Sweden: [go̱hth-en-burg], first syllable to rhyme with *oath*, and [go̱t-en-burg], first syllable the same as *got*, are rather old-fashioned, and, to-day, people usually make some attempt at the Swedish name, which is not pronounced in a manner at all obvious to the Englishman.

GOUGE: [gooj], to rhyme with *stooge*. OR [gouj].

GOUROCK, Scotland: [go̯o̯ə-rok], first syllable to rhyme with many people's pronunciation of *poor*. NOT [go̯u̯-wə-rok], first part the same as *Gower*.

GOVAN, Scotland: [gʌv-ən], the same as *govern*. NOT [go̱hv-ən], first syllable rhyming with *stove*.

GOVERNESS: [gʌv-nis], two syllables. But [gʌv-ə-nis], three, is sometimes heard.

GOVERNMENT: [gʌv-ə-mənt], no first N. OR [gʌv-ən-mənt], with first N; this latter pronunciation would certainly be used when making a speech.

GOVERNOR: [gʌv-nə], two syllables—of a school, etc. This pronunciation or, more usually, its abbreviation *guv* [gʌv], is also used by the London working-classes in situations in which they would have formerly said *Sir! The Governor*—also with this same pronunciation [gʌv-nə]—was, a long time ago, used by the U to refer to their fathers. Then the expression became non-U; it has now died out. (*Pater* or *The Pater*, also meaning 'father', has suffered a similar fate: it was once U, became non-U, and died out.) Note that the governor of a steam-engine is [gʌv-ə-nə], three syllables.

GRADUATE: [grad-yʊ-wit], first syllable to rhyme with *bad*; or [graj-yʊ-wit], first syllable to rhyme with *badge*, as a noun; but as a verb [grad-yʊ-wayt], [graj-yʊ-wayt], last syllable the same as *wait*.

GRAHAM, surname: [gram], the same as *gramme*. OR [gray-əm], to rhyme with *pay 'em* (i.e. *pay them*).

GRANADA, Spain—but better known from *Granada Television*: [grə-nah-də], accent on second syllable. NOT [gran-ə-də], accent on first.

GRANARD, peer's title: [gran-əd], to rhyme with *mannered*. NOT [grən-ahd], accent on second syllable.

GRANDTULLY, Scotland: [grahnt-il], first syllable to rhyme with *can't*.

GRANT: [grahnt], to rhyme with *can't*. NOT [grant], rhyming with *cant*.

GRANTHAM: [grahn-təm], first syllable to rhyme with *barn*. NOT [gran-thəm], rhyming with *anthem*.

GRAPH: [graf], to rhyme with *gaff*. NOT [grahf], rhyming with *scarf*.

GRASP: [grahsp]. NOT [grasp].

GREASY: [gree-si], to rhyme with *fleecy*; but [gree-zi], to rhyme with *easy*, is often heard.

GREENGAGE: [green-gayj], the two syllables being equally stressed. OR [green-gayj], accent on first syllable.

GREENOCK, town in Scotland: [gren-ək], first syllable to rhyme with *ten*.

GREENWICH: [grin-ij], first syllable the same as *grin*, second to rhyme with *bridge*. The pronunciation [gren-ich], first syllable to rhyme with *ten*, second the same as *itch*, is often heard. So also is [grin-ich].

GRENADA. Most Englishmen say [grə-nahd-ə], second syllable to rhyme with *hard*. But in the West Indies the island is called [grə-nayd-ə], first part the same as *grenade*. NOT [gren-ə-də], accent on first syllable.

GRENOBLE, France: [grə-noh-bəl], last part the same as *noble*. To use the French pronunciation would be affected.

GRIEVOUS: [greev-əs], to rhyme with *leave us!* NOT [greev-i-yəs], three syllables.

GRIFFITHS, Welsh surname: [grif-is], no TH. NOT [grif-iths], with TH.

GROOM: [grʊm], to rhyme with first syllable of *woman*. NOT [groom], rhyming with *boom*.

GROSVENOR *Square*: [groh-və-nə], no S.

GUILFOYLE, Irish surname: [gil-foil], accent on first syllable. NOT [gil-foil], accent on second.

GUNWALE, nautical: [gʌn-əl], to rhyme with *funnel*. NOT [gʌn-wayl], the same as *gun+whale*.

GURKHA: [gu̱rk-ə], to rhyme with *worker*; [go̱o̱ə-kə], first syllable to rhyme with many people's pronunciation of *poor*, is now not much used.

GUYANA: [gɛi-ya̱ẖ-nə], first syllable to rhyme with *buy*; formerly *British* GUIANA which, in England, was pronounced [gee-ya̱ẖ-nə], first syllable to rhyme with *bee*.

GYNAECOLOGY: [jɛin-ə-ko̱l-ə-ji] with initial [j]. OR [gɛin-ə-ko̱l-ə-ji] with initial [g].

GYROSCOPE: mostly [jɛi̱ə-rə-skohp] with initial [j], but sometimes [gɛi̱ə-rə-skohp] with initial [g].

HAITI: [ha̱y-ti], to rhyme with *Katie*. NOT [hah-e̱e̱-ti], accent on second syllable, rhyming with *Tahiti*.

HAKLUYT, surname: [ha̱k-lit], two syllables, second the same as *lit*. NOT [ha̱k-lʊ-wit], three syllables.

HALFPENNY: [ha̱y-pen-i], first syllable the same as *hay*. NOT [ha̱ẖf-pen-i], as spelt.

HALT: [hawlt]. NOT [holt].

HALTER: [ha̱wl-tə], first syllable the same as *haul*. NOT [ho̱l-tə], first syllable rhyming with *doll*.

HANDKERCHIEF: [ha̱ng-kə-chif], first syllable to rhyme with *bang*, or [hɛng-kə-chif]; last syllable to rhyme with *sniff*. NOT [ha̱ng-kə-cheef], or [hɛng-kə-cheef], last syllable the same as *chief*; or [ha̱ng-kə-cheev], or [hɛng-kə-cheev], last syllable rhyming with *heave*.

HANG: [heng], or [hang], to rhyme with *bang*. NOT [hengg], [hangg], with final G.

HANGAR: [heng-ə], or [hang-ə], first syllable to rhyme with *bang*. NOT [heng-gə], or [hang-gə].

HANOVER: [han-o-və], accent on first syllable. NOT the German pronunciation.

HAREM: [hɛə-rəm], to rhyme with *scare 'em* (i.e. *scare them*). OR [hə-reem], accent on second syllable.

HAREWOOD, peer's title: [hah-wʊd], first syllable to rhyme with *bar*. NOT [hɛə-wʊd], as spelt.

HARLECH, Wales: [hah-lek].

HARTLEPOOL: [haht-li-pool], first part to rhyme with *partly*. NOT [haht-əl-pool], first part rhyming with *startle*.

HARWICH: [har-ij], to rhyme with *carriage*.

HASP: [hahsp]. NOT [hasp].

HATCHARD, surname, known from the name of a London book-seller: [hach-ahd], second syllable to rhyme with *hard*. NOT [hach-əd], second syllable the same as that of *dullard*.

HAULM: [hawm], to rhyme with *norm*. OR [hahm], the same as *harm*.

HAUNCH: [hawnch], to rhyme with *paunch*. The pronunciation [hahnch], to rhyme with *branch*, is rather old-fashioned.

HAWAII: [hə-wɛi-i], second syllable the same as *why*, is now more usual than [hə-way-i], second syllable the same as *way*.

HAWARDEN, Flintshire—Gladstone lived for long in the Castle here: [hahd-ən], the same as *harden*.

HAWICK, Scotland: [hoik], one syllable.

HAWORTH, Yorkshire: [hou̯-wəth], first syllable the same as *how*. NOT [hay̱-wəth], first syllable the same as *hay*.

HEATHCOTE, surname: [heth-kət], first syllable to rhyme with *death*. NOT [heeth-kət], first syllable the same as *heath*.

HEDGEHOG: [hej-og], no second H, accent on first syllable. NOT [hej-hog], with second H, the two syllables being equally stressed.

HEIGHT: [hεit], to rhyme with *right*. NOT [hεitth].

HEINOUS: [hayn-əs], first syllable to rhyme with *Dane*. NOT [hεin-əs], first syllable rhyming with *dine*, or [heen-əs], first syllable rhyming with *dean*.

HEIRESS: [εə-res], accent on first syllable. NOT [εə-res], accent on second.

HELENA, Christian name: [hel-ə-nə], accent on first syllable, to rhyme with *Eleanor*. OR [həl-een-ə], accent on second.

HELICOPTER: [hel-i-kop-tə], first syllable the same as *hell*. NOT [heel-i-kop-tə], first syllable the same as *heel*.

HELIOTROPE: [hel-yə-trohp], first syllable the same as *hell*. NOT [heel-yə-trohp], first syllable the same as *heel*.

HELLO! The word has many different intonations and pronunciations; for instance, [həl-oh], to rhyme with *below*; [hal-oh], first syllable to rhyme with *pal*; [hʌl-oh], first syllable to rhyme with *dull*; [hel-oh], first syllable the same as *hell*; [hloh], one syllable.

HELSINKI: [hel-sing-ki], accent on first syllable. NOT [hel-sing-ki], accent on the second. This Finnish name of the town is now more used than its Swedish name, HELSINGFORS, which used to be normal in England; this last is pronounced [hel-sing-fawz] by the English, which is not the way the Swedes pronounce it.

HELVELLYN, mountain in Cumberland: [hel-vel-yən].

HENEAGE, surname: [hen-ij], first syllable the same as *hen*. NOT [heen-ij], first syllable rhyming with *seen*.

HERMIONE, Christian name: [hə-mei-yə-ni], accent on second syllable. NOT [hə-mi-yoh-ni], accent on third.

HERO: [heeə-roh], first syllable the same as *hear*. NOT [hee-roh], first syllable the same as *he*.

HERSTMONCEUX, Sussex: [hurst-mon-soo], accent on first syllable, last syllable to rhyme with *do*.

HERTFORD: [hah-fəd], first syllable to rhyme with *car*, no T. NOT [haht-fəd], first syllable the same as *heart*, still less [hurt-fəd], first syllable the same as *hurt*.

HIDEOUS: [hid-yəs], first syllable the same as *hid*; the old pronunciation [hij-əs], first syllable to rhyme with *bridge*, is not often heard.

HIMALAYAS: [hi-mə-lay-yəz], accent on third syllable, which is the same as *lay*. NOT [hi-mahl-ə-yəz], accent on second syllable, which is the same as *marl*.

HIROSHIMA: [hi-rosh-im-ə], accent on second syllable; this is not the Japanese pronunciation.

HIVES, skin eruption: [hɛivz], to rhyme with *thrives*. NOT [hɛi-veez], rhyming with *Dives* (Bible).

HOLBEACH, Lincolnshire: [hohl-beech], first syllable the same as *whole*. NOT [hol-beech], first syllable rhyming with *doll*.

HOLBORN, London: [hoh-bən], first syllable the same as *hoe*, no L.

HOLSTER: [hohl-stə], first syllable the same as *hole*. NOT [hol-stə], first syllable rhyming with *doll*.

HOLYHEAD: [hol-i-hed], first syllable to rhyme with *doll*. NOT [hohl-i-hed], first two syllables the same as *holy*.

HOLYROOD *Palace*: [hol-i-rood], first two syllables the same as *holly*. NOT as spelt.

HOLYWELL, street in Oxford: [hol-i-wel], first two syllables the same as *holly*. NOT as spelt.

HOMAGE: [hom-ij], with H. OR [om-ij], without H.

HOME, peer's title: [hyoom], to rhyme with *fume*. NOT [hohm], the same as *home*.

HOMOSEXUAL: [hom-o-sɛk-syʋ-wəl], first syllable to rhyme with *Tom*. OR [hohm-o-sɛk-syʋ-wəl], first syllable the same as *home*.

HONDURAS: [hon-dyʋ-rəs], accent on first syllable. OR [hon-dyaw-rəs], accent on second. I myself use the first pronunciation for the Republic of Honduras, the second for British Honduras.

HONITON, Devon: [hon-i-tən], first syllable to rhyme with *on*. NOT [hʌn-i-tən], first syllable the same as *Hun*.

104

HOOF: [hʊf]. NOT [hoof]; but the latter pronunciation when, in a rather old-fashioned manner, the word is used as a verb (*Hoof him out!*).

HOOP: [hoop], to rhyme with *droop*. But some old croquet-players say [hʊp].

HORNCASTLE, Lincolnshire: [ha̱w̱n-ka̱ẖs-əl], the first two syllables being equally stressed. NOT [ha̱w̱n-kahs-əl], accent only on the first.

HORRIBLE: [ho̱r-i-bəl]. The pronunciation [o̱r-i-bəl], no H, is a joke.

HORS-D'ŒUVRE. Pronounced in the French way. The pronunciation [ha̱ws doo-və], is an ancient joke—an attempt by the U at what they think the non-U would say.

HORSHAM, Sussex: [ha̱w̱-shəm]. NOT [ha̱ws-əm], first syllable the same as *horse*.

HOSPITABLE: [ho̱s-pit-ə-bəl], accent on first syllable. NOT [hos-pi̱t-ə-bəl], accent on second.

HOSPITAL: [ho̱s-pit-əl]. The pronunciation [a̱ws-pit-əl], no H and first syllable to rhyme with *force*, was once U, but would now sound dialectal.

HOSTESS: [ho̱ẖ-stis], accent on first syllable. NOT [hoh-ste̱s], accent on second, rhyming with *dress*.

HOTEL: [hoh-te̱l], with H. [oh-te̱l], without H, is old-fashioned, but is still sometimes heard from old U-people. Naturally those who use the latter pronunciation say (and write) *an hotel*, not *a hotel*.

HOUGH, surname: [hʌf], the same as *huff*. OR [hou], the same as *how*.

HOUSTON, U.S.A. The American pronunciation is [hyǫǫ-stən], first syllable the same as *Hugh*.

HOUSEWIFERY: [hous-wif̲-ə-ri], accent on second syllable, which rhymes with *sniff*. OR [hous-węif-ri], three syllables, as spelt. The pronunciations [hʌz-if-ri], [hʌz-wif-ri], accent on first syllable, which rhymes with *buzz*, are probably dead, but a pronunciation parallel to the first of these may still exist:- HOUSEWIFE, meaning 'little case containing needles, etc.', as [hʌz-if]. But in its normal meaning *housewife* is pronounced as spelt.

HOVEL: [họv-el], to rhyme with *novel*. OR [hʌv-əl], to rhyme with *shovel*.

HOWTH, Ireland: [hohdh], to rhyme with *loathe*. NOT [houth], rhyming with *mouth*.

HUMBLE: [hʌm-bəl], with H. [ʌm-bəl], without H, well known in Dickens' time, must now be considered dead.

HUMOUR: [hyǫǫ-mə], with H. [yǫǫ-mə], without H, is perhaps rather old-fashioned. Similarly GOOD-HUMOURED, etc.

HUNSTANTON, Norfolk. The older pronunciation is [hʌn-stən], two syllables, to rhyme with *Dunstan*, but the three-syllabled [hʌn-sta̲n-tən], accent on the second syllable, is gaining ground.

HUSSAR: [həz-a̲h], to rhyme with *bazaar*, is now more used than [hʊz-a̲h].

HYDERABAD, India: [hɛi-drə-ba̲d], three syllables, accent on last.

106

HYDRANGEA: [hɛi-drayn-jə], second syllable the same as *drain*. NOT [hɛi-dran-jə], second syllable rhyming with *can*.

HYDRAULIC: [hɛi-drawl-ik], second syllable the same as *drawl*. OR [hei-drol-ik], second syllable to rhyme with *doll*.

HYPOCRITICAL: [hip-ə-krit-i-kəl], first syllable to rhyme with *rip*. NOT [hɛip-ə-krit-i-kəl], first syllable rhyming with *ripe*, for this is the pronunciation of *hypercritical*.

IBADAN, Nigeria: [i-bad-ən], accent on second syllable. OR [i-bəd-an], accent on third.

IDEAL: [ɛi-dee-yəl], three syllables. NOT [ɛi-deel], two, second the same as *deal*.

IDYLL: [id-il], first syllable to rhyme with *bid*. OR [ɛid-il], first syllable to rhyme with *bide*. Similarly IDYLLIC.

ILKESTON, Derbyshire: [il-kə-stən], three syllables. NOT [ilk-stən], two.

ILKLEY, Yorkshire: [ilk-li]. But in the song, *On Ilkley Moor baht 'at*—*baht* means 'without'—it is [ilk-lə], sometimes spelt *Ilkla'*, a Yorkshire pronunciation.

ILLUMINATE: [i-loom-in-ayt], second syllable to rhyme with *boom*. OR [i-lyoom-in-ayt], second syllable to rhyme with *fume*.

ILLUSION: [i-loozh-ən], second syllable to rhyme with *rouge*. OR [i-lyoozh-ən].

IMPIOUS: [imp-i-yəs], accent on first syllable. NOT [im-pɛi-yəs], accent on second, last part the same as *pious*.

107

IMPORTUNE: [im-paw-tyoon], accent on second syllable. OR [im-paw-tyoon], accent on third.

IMPOT, school slang: [im-pot], with T; facetious [im-poh], without T.

INCHIQUIN, peer's title: [inch-kwin], two syllables. NOT [inch-i-kwin], three.

INCHOATE: [in-ko-wət], accent on first syllable. NOT [in-koh-wət], accent on second.

INCOGNITO: [in-kog-ni-toh], accent on second syllable. [in-kog-neet-oh], accent on third, which is the same as *neat*, is often heard.

INCOMPARABLE: [in-kom-pər-ə-bəl], accent on second syllable. NOT [in-kəm-pεə-rə-bəl], accent on third. Similarly INCOMPARABLY: [in-kom-pər-ə-bli]. NOT [in-kəm-pεə-rə-bli].

INDIANA: [in-di-yahn-ə], third syllable to rhyme with *barn*. But the American pronunciation is [in-dee-yan-ə], third syllable to rhyme with *ban*.

INEXORABLE: [in-εks-ə-rə-bəl], accent on second syllable. NOT [in-ek-zaw-rə-bəl], accent on third.

INEXTRICABLE: [in-εks-trik-ə-bəl], accent on second syllable. OR [in-eks-trik-ə-bəl], accent on third.

INFILTRATE: [in-fil-trayt], accent on first syllable. NOT [in-fil-trayt], accent on second.

INGE, surname: [ing], to rhyme with *sing*. NOT [inj], rhyming with *singe*.

INGLIS, Scotch surname: [ing-gəlz], to rhyme with *shingles*. NOT as spelt.

INHERENT: [in-heeə-rənt], second syllable the same as *hear*. NOT [in-he-rənt], last part rhyming with *errant*.

INTERESTING: [in-tres-ting], three syllables, accent on the first. NOT [in-tər-es-ting], four syllables, accent on the third.

INTERLUDE: [in-tə-lood], last syllable to rhyme with *rude*. OR [in-tə-lyood], last syllable to rhyme with *feud*.

INTESTINAL: [in-tes-tein-əl], accent on third syllable. NOT [in-tes-tin-əl], accent on second.

INVALID, noun: [in-və-leed], last syllable to rhyme with *read*. OR [in-və-lid], last syllable the same as *lid*. Accent on first syllable. But the adjective—meaning 'not valid'—is [in-val-id], accent on second.

INVEIGLE: [in-vee-gəl], second syllable to rhyme with *pea*. OR [in-vay-gəl], second syllable to rhyme with *pay*.

INVOLVED: [in-volvd]. NOT [in-vohlvd].

IODINE: [ɛi-yo-deen], last syllable the same as *dean*. [ɛi-yo-dein], last syllable the same as *dine*, is old-fashioned.

IOWA: [ɛi-yoh-wə], accent on first syllable. NOT [ɛi-yoh-wə], accent on second.

IRAN: [i-rahn], second syllable to rhyme with *barn*. OR [i-ran], second syllable the same as *ran*.

IRASCIBLE: [i-ras-i-bəl] or [ɛi-ras-i-bəl], without C. NOT [i-ras-ki-bəl] or [ɛi-ras-ki-bel], with C.

IRENE, Christian name: [ɛi-reen-i], three syllables, accent on the second. NOT [ɛi-reen], two syllables, accent on the first, which is American.

IRREPARABLE: [i-rep-rə-bəl], four syllables, accent on second. NOT [i-rə-peɛ-rə-bəl], five syllables, accent on third.

IRREVOCABLE: [i-rev-ə-kə-bəl], accent on second syllable. NOT [i-ri-voh-kə-bəl], accent on third.

ISHAM, surname: [ɛi-shəm]. NOT [ish-əm], first syllable rhyming with *fish*.

ISMAY, surname: [iz-may], first syllable the same as *is*. NOT [is-may], first syllable rhyming with *hiss*.

ISN'T IT?: [iz-ənt it]. NOT [i-də-nit]; or [i-nit], two syllables, rhyming with *linnet*.

ISSUE: [is-yʊ], first syllable to rhyme with *hiss*. OR [ish-yʊ], first syllable to rhyme with *fish*.

IVEAGH, Irish surname: [ɛiv-ə], to rhyme with *fiver*.

JACKASS: [jak-as], second syllable to rhyme with *gas*. OR [jak-ahs], second syllable to rhyme with *farce*.

JAMB, of a door, etc.: [jam], the same as *jam*, no B. NOT [jamb], with B.

JAMESON, Irish surname: [jem-i-sən], three syllables, first the same as *gem*. NOT [jaym-sən], as spelt.

JAMIESON, Scotch surname: [jim-i-sən], first syllable the same as *Jim*. NOT [jaym-i-sən], as spelt.

110

JAQUES, surname: [jayks], to rhyme with *cakes*.

JARDINE, surname: [jah-d<u>ee</u>n], accent on second syllable, which is the same as *dean*. NOT [jah-d<u>i</u>n], as spelt.

JASMINE: [j<u>a</u>z-min], first syllable to rhyme with *has*. OR [j<u>a</u>s-min], first syllable to rhyme with *gas*.

JASPER: [j<u>a</u>s-pə], first syllable to rhyme with *gas*. [j<u>ah</u>s-pə], first syllable to rhyme with *farce*, is old-fashioned.

JAUNDICE: [j<u>aw</u>n-dis], first syllable to rhyme with *born*. [j<u>ah</u>n-dis], first syllable to rhyme with *barn*, is now no longer heard.

JEDBURGH, Scotland: [j<u>e</u>d-brə], second syllable the same as the last syllable of *Edinburgh*.

JEKYLL, surname, known from Robert Louis Stevenson's *Strange Case of Dr. Jekyll and Mr. Hyde*: [j<u>ee</u>k-il], first syllable to rhyme with *cheek*. OR [j<u>e</u>k-il], first syllable to rhyme with *check*.

JEROME, saint's name: [j<u>e</u>-rohm], accent on first syllable. NOT [jə-r<u>oh</u>m], accent on second. But this latter is the pronunciation of the name of the author *Jerome K. Jerome*, who wrote *Three Men in a Boat*. NOT [jə-r<u>oh</u>m-i], three syllables.

JERVAULX *Abbey*, Yorkshire: [j<u>ur</u>-voh], to rhyme with *servo-* (as in *servo-mechanism*).

JERVIS, surname. Some of its bearers call it [j<u>ur</u>-vis], to rhyme with *service*, others [j<u>ah</u>-vis], first syllable to rhyme with *car*.

JEWEL: [jool], one syllable, to rhyme with *pool*. OR [j<u>oo</u>-wəl], two syllables.

JOB, Bible: [johb], to rhyme with *robe*. NOT [job], the same as *job*.

JOCOSE: [jək-o̱hs], second syllable to rhyme with *dose*. NOT [jək-o̱hz], second syllable rhyming with *doze*.

JOULE, surname: [joul], the same as *jowl*. The unit of work of this name (= .7375 foot-pounds) is called after an English physicist, but scientists often pronounce this [jool], to rhyme with *fool*, because they have lost sight of the origin of the name and feel it to be foreign.

JOWETT, surname. The celebrated Master of Balliol was called [jo̱h-wit]; in a verse, his name rhymes with *stow it!*

JUMNA, river in India: [jʌm-nə], first syllable to rhyme with *rum*.

JURA, France: [ja̱w-rə], to rhyme with *Laura*. NOT the French pronunciation.

JUST, adverb: [jest], to rhyme with *rest*. OR [jʌst], to rhyme with *rust*—and this latter is the only pronunciation of JUST, adjective.

KABUL, Afghanistan: [ka̱w-bəl], to rhyme with *bauble*. NOT [kə-bṳl], accent on second syllable, which is the same as *bull*.

KANO, Nigeria: [ka̱hn-oh]. First syllable to rhyme with *barn*. NOT [ka̱yn-oh], first syllable the same as *cane*.

KARLSBAD = *Karlovy Vary*, Czecho-Slovakia: [ka̱hlz-bad], second syllable the same as *bad*.

112

KASHMIR: [kash-me͙e͙ə], accent on second syllable. But, when applied to a shawl, it is written *cashmere* and pronounced [ka͙sh-meeə], accent on first syllable.

KAVANAGH, Irish surname: [ka͙v-ə-nə], accent on first syllable. NOT [kə-va͙n-ə], rhyming with *savannah*.

KEDGEREE: [kej-er-e͙e͙], accent on last syllable. OR [ke͙j-er-i], accent on first.

KEIGHLEY, Yorkshire: [ke͙e͙th-li], first syllable to rhyme with *teeth*.

KEIR, surname: [keeə], to rhyme with *dear*.

KENYA: [ke͙e͙n-yə], first syllable the same as *keen*. OR [ke͙n-yə], first syllable the same as *ken*.

KEOGH, Irish surname: [ke͙e͙-yoh], to rhyme with *Leo*.

KESWICK, Cumberland: [ke͙z-ik], no W, first syllable to rhyme with *fez*.

KETELBY, surname of the composer of light music: [kə-te͙l-bi], accent on second syllable. NOT [ke͙t-əl-bi], accent on first.

KEYNES, surname: [kaynz], the same as *canes*. NOT [keenz], rhyming with *cleans*.

KIEV: [ke͙e͙-yef], two syllables. NOT [keev], rhyming with *grieve*.

KILGOUR, Scotch surname: [kil-go͙u-wə], last part the same as *Gower*; accent on second syllable. NOT [kil-go͙o͙ə], second syllable rhyming with many people's pronunciation of *poor*.

113

KILMOREY, peer's title: [kil-mʌr-i], accent on second syllable, last part the same as *Murray*. NOT [kil-mawr-i], last part rhyming with *story*.

KILOMETRE: [kil-o-mee-tə], accent on first syllable. NOT [kil-o-mi-tə], accent on second.

KINCAID, surname: [kin-kayd], accent on second syllable.

KINETIC: [ki-net-ik], second syllable the same as *net*. NOT [kɛi-neet-ik], second syllable the same as *neat*, first rhyming with *buy*.

KINGUSSIE, Scotland: [king-yoos-i], second syllable the same as *use* (noun). NOT [kin-gʌs-i], as spelt.

KIOSK: [kee-yosk], accent on first syllable, which is the same as *key*. NOT [kɛi-yosk], first syllable rhyming with *buy*; or [ki-yosk], accent on second syllable.

KIRKCALDY, Scotland. The Scotch pronunciation is [kə-kod-i], no L. But, when it is a surname, Englishmen usually pronounce it [kə-kawl-di], second syllable the same as *call*.

KIRKCUDBRIGHT: [kə-koo-bri], no D, no T.

KNOLL: [nohl], to rhyme with *dole*. NOT [nol], rhyming with *doll*.

KNOLLYS, peer's title: [nohlz], to rhyme with *holes*. NOT [nol-is], two syllables, rhyming with *Dollis* (*Hill*).

KNOWLEDGE: [nol-ij], first syllable to rhyme with *doll*. NOT [nohl-ij], first syllable rhyming with *dole*.

114

KRAKÓW, Poland: [krak̲-ou], accent on first syllable. OR [krə-kou̲], accent on second.

KUALA LUMPUR: [kwah̲l-ə lʌmp-ə], third syllable the same as *lump*.

LABORATORY: [lə-bo̲r-at-ri], accent on second syllable. NOT [lab̲-rə-tə-ri], accent on first.

LACUNA: [lə-kyo̲o̲-nə], second syllable to rhyme with *dew*. NOT [lə-ko̲o̲-nə], second syllable rhyming with *do*.

LAGOS, Nigeria: [lay̲g-os], first syllable to rhyme with *vague*.

LAING, Scotch surname: [layng]. But it has often been pronounced [lang]—thus as if spelt *Lang*—by Englishmen.

LAMENTABLE: [lam̲-ən-təb-əl], accent on first syllable. NOT [lə-me̲nt-ə-bəl], accent on second.

LAMING, surname. Usually [lay̲m-ing], to rhyme with *blaming*. But sometimes [lam̲-ing], to rhyme with *damning*.

LAMPETER, Wales: [lam̲-pi-tə], accent on first syllable.

LANARK: [lan̲-ək], to rhyme with *bannock*. NOT [lə-nah̲k], accent on second syllable.

LANDAU: [lan-da̲w], accent on second syllable, which rhymes with *caw*; or [lan̲-daw], accent on first syllable. NOT [lan-do̲u], or [lan̲-dou], second syllable rhyming with *cow*.

LANDSCAPE: [lan̲-skip], second syllable to rhyme with *ship*, no D. OR [lan̲d-skayp], second syllable to rhyme with *shape*, with D.

115

LANOLIN: [lạn-o-lin], last syllable to rhyme with *sin*. OR [lạn-o-leen], last syllable to rhyme with *seen*.

LAOS: [lous], the same as *louse*. NOT [lạy-yos], two syllables, first the same as *lay*.

LASCELLES, surname: [lạs-əlz], to rhyme with *tassels*. NOT [ləs-ẹlz], accent on second syllable.

LAST: [lahst]. NOT [last], rhyming with *gassed*.

LAS VEGAS: [las vẹeg-əs], second syllable to rhyme with *league*. OR [las vạyg-əs], second syllable the same as *vague*.

LATHAM, surname: [lạydh-əm], first syllable the same as *lathe*. NOT [lạth-əm], first syllable rhyming with *hath*.

LATHER: [lạ-dhə], to rhyme with *gather*. NOT [lạh-dhə], rhyming with *father*. This second, non-U pronunciation is almost universal in the television advertisements for soap-powders, etc. There are, however, occasional U advertising announcers. These feel [lạh-dhə] to be wrong and [lạ-dhə] to be unintelligible to the viewers, so they compromise by using an un-English vowel in the first syllable, namely that of German *mann*.

LAUDANUM: [lọd-nəm], two syllables, first to rhyme with *rod*. NOT [lạwd-ə-nəm], three syllables, first rhyming with *roared*. But the word is obsolete.

LAUGHTER: [lạhf-tə], first syllable to rhyme with *scarf*. NOT [lạf-tə], first syllable rhyming with *gaff*.

LAUNCH, noun and verb: Navy and old-fashioned U [lahnch]; otherwise [lawnch], to rhyme with *paunch*.

LAUNDRY: [lawn-dri], first syllable the same as *lawn*. [lahn-dri], first syllable to rhyme with *barn*, is very old-fashioned U.

LAVERY, surname. Usually [layv-ər-i], first syllable to rhyme with *save*. OR [lav-ər-i], first syllable to rhyme with *have*.

LEAMINGTON: [lem-ing-tən], first syllable to rhyme with *hem*.

LECTURE: [lek-chə], the combination [kch] being the same as *ckch* in *deck-chair*. NOT [lek-shə], the combination [ksh] being the same as *cks* in *cocksure*.

LEGEND: [lej-ənd], first syllable the same as *ledge*. NOT [leej-ənd], first syllable the same as *liege*.

LEGHORN = *Livorno*, Italy: [lə-gawn], accent on second syllable, no H.

LEIGHTON *Buzzard*, Bedfordshire: [layt-ən], to rhyme with *Drayton*.

LEISURE: [lezh-ə]. NOT [leezh-ə].

LEITRIM, Ireland: [leet-rim], first syllable to rhyme with *beat*. NOT [layt-rim], first syllable the same as *late*.

LE MANS, France: [lə-manz], second syllable the same as *man's*. OR the French pronunciation.

LEMUR: [leem-ə], to rhyme with *steamer*. OR [lem-ə], the same as *lemma*.

LENGTH: [length]. NOT [lenth], no G, rhyming with *tenth*.

LENINGRAD: [len-in-grad], last syllable to rhyme with *bad*. OR [len-in-grahd], last syllable to rhyme with *bard*. Accent on first syllable.

117

LEOMINSTER, Herefordshire: [lem-stə], two syllables, first to rhyme with *hem*.

LE QUEUX, surname: [lə-kyoo], second syllable the same as *cue*.

LERWICK, Shetlands: [lur-wik], first syllable to rhyme with *burr*. NOT [le-rik], rhyming with *Eric*.

LETTUCE: [let-is], second syllable to rhyme with *hiss*. NOT [let-ʌs], the same as *Let us—*.

Loch LEVEN: [leev-ən], to rhyme with *even*. NOT [lev-ən], rhyming with *heaven*.

LEVERHULME, peer's title: [lee-və-hyoom], last syllable to rhyme with *fume*.

LEVESON-GOWER, surname: [loos-ən gaw], first part the same as *loosen*, second the same as *gore*.

LEVIN, surname. Often [lə-veen], accent on second syllable, which rhymes with *been*.

LICHEN: [leik-ən], the same as *liken*. OR [lich-in], to rhyme with *kitchen*.

LICORICE: [lik-ə-rəs]. The pronunciation [lik-ə-rish], third syllable rhyming with *dish*, is probably now only dialectal.

LIDO: [leed-oh], first syllable to rhyme with *feed*. NOT [leid-oh], rhyming with *Fido*.

In LIEU: [loo], to rhyme with *do*. NOT [lyoo], rhyming with *dew*.

LIEUTENANT. The word is pronounced [lef-ten-ənt], with [f], in the Army and by most people, but [lə-ten-ənt], no [f], in

118

the Navy. The American pronunciation is [loo-tẹn-ənt], first
syllable the same as *loo*.

LINLITHGOW, Scotland: [lin-lịth-goh], last syllable the same as
go. NOT [lin-lịth-gou], last syllable rhyming with *cow*.

LISLE, surname: [lɛil], to rhyme with *pile*.

LISTOWEL, Ireland: [lis-tọh-wəl], second syllable to rhyme with
hoe. NOT [lis-tọu-wəl], second syllable rhyming with *how*.

LLANDOVERY, Wales: [lan-dʌv-ri], three syllables, second the
same as *dove*.

LLANDRINDOD *Wells*, Wales: [lan-drịn-dəd], accent on second
syllable. NOT [lan-drin-dọd], accent on third.

LLANDUDNO: [lan-dịd-noh], second syllable the same as *did*.
OR [lan-dʌd-noh], second syllable the same as *dud*.

LLANELLY: [lan-ẹth-li], last part to rhyme with *deathly*. NOT
the Welsh pronunciation.

LLANGOLLEN, Wales: [lan-gọth-lin], second syllable the same
as *Goth*.

LLEYN *Peninsula*, Wales: [leen], the same as *lean*.

LOCKERBIE, Scotland: [lọk-ə-bi], accent on first syllable.

LOCUS: [lọhk-əs], to rhyme with *crocus*. [lọk-əs], first syllable
the same as *lock*, is 'more correct'.

LOFOTEN *Islands*: [lof-ọh-tən], accent on second syllable. OR
[lọf-o-tən], accent on first.

119

LOFT: [lawft], to rhyme with *dwarfed*. OR [loft] to rhyme with *scoffed*.

LOMBARDY: [lʌm-bə-di], first syllable to rhyme with *rum*. But [lọm-bə-di], first syllable to rhyme with *Tom*, is often heard, LOMBARD meaning 'inhabitant of Lombardy' (also as an adjective)—the word occurs in *Lombard Street* too—usually has [lọm-].

LONDONDERRY: [lʌn-dən-der-i], accent on first syllable. But the Irish call it [lʌn-dən-dẹr-i], the first and third syllables being equally stressed.

LONGEVITY: [lon-jẹv-it-i], first syllable to rhyme with *don*, second with *rev*. But the first syllable is often the same as *long*, and the second may rhyme with *leave*, so that [lon-jẹẹv-it-i], [long-jẹv-it-i] and [long-jẹẹv-it-i] can also be heard.

LONGITUDE. The official pronunciation appears to be [lọnj-i-tyood], with [j]. Many people, however, say [lọng-gi-tyood], with [g]; and some [lọng-ti-tyood], with an inserted T (because of *latitude*?).

LOOK: [lʊk]. NOT [look].

LORRY. The old U-pronunciation [lʌ-ri], to rhyme with *curry*, used before lorries were motor-lorries, is still heard. But most people say [lọ-ri], to rhyme with *sorry*.

LOS ALAMOS, U.S.A.: [los ạl-ə-mos], accent on first syllable of second word.

LOSS: [laws], to rhyme with *force*. OR [los], to rhyme with *Ross*.

LOUDOUN, peeress's title: [lọu̯-dən], the same as *louden* meaning 'to make louder'. NOT [lʊ-dọọn], accent on second syllable.

LOUGHBOROUGH: [lʌf-bər-ə], first syllable to rhyme with *stuff*.

LOUGHTON, Essex: [lou̯-tən], first syllable to rhyme with *cow*.

LOVAT, surname: [lʌv-ət], first syllable the same as *love*.

LOVE: [lʌv]. Naturally the word often occurs in songs. It is not possible to sing the sound [ʌ] on a long note, so the singer automatically turns the word into [lurv], to rhyme with *swerve*. This pronunciation, [lurv], was used as a joke in the twenties.

LOWELL, surname: [loh-wəl], first syllable to rhyme with *go*. NOT [lou̯-wəl], rhyming with *trowel*.

LOWESTOFT: [loh-wis-tawft], last syllable to rhyme with *dwarfed*. OR [loh-wis-toft], last syllable to rhyme with *scoffed*.

LUCERNE: [lʊ-surn], accent on second syllable.

LUCID: [loo-sid], first syllable to rhyme with *do*. OR [lyoo-sid], first syllable to rhyme with *dew*.

LUCRATIVE: [loo-krə-tiv], first syllable to rhyme with *do*. OR [lyoo-krə-tiv], first syllable to rhyme with *dew*.

LUCUBRATION: [lʊ-kyʊ-bray-shən]. OR [lʊ-kʊ-bray-shən].

LUKEWARM: [lʊk-wawm], [look-wawm], or [lyook-wawm] (first syllable to rhyme with *duke*).

LUTE: [loot], the same as *loot*. OR [lyoot], to rhyme with *newt*.

LUTYENS, surname of the architect: [lʌt-yənz], first syllable to rhyme with *but*. NOT [lʊt-yənz], first syllable rhyming with *put*; or [loot-yənz], first syllable rhyming with *boot*.

LUXEMBOURG: [lʌk-səm-burg], first syllable the same as *luck*. OR [lʊk-səm-burg], first syllable the same as *look*.

LUXURIANT: [lʌks-ya̲w-ri-yənt], first syllable to rhyme with *tucks*. OR [lʌgz-ya̲w-ri-yənt], first syllable to rhyme with *tugs*.

LYCIDAS: [li̲s-i-das], first syllable to rhyme with *hiss*.

LYLY, author's name: [li̲-li], the same as *lily*. NOT [lɛi-lɛi], each syllable rhyming with *buy*.

LYMPNE, Kent: [lim], the same as *limb*.

LYONS = *Lyon*, France: [lahnz], to rhyme with *barns*. OR [lɛiənz], to rhyme with some people's pronunciation of *irons*.

LYSAGHT, Irish surname: [lɛi̲s-aht], first syllable the same as *lice*, second the same as *art*.

LYTHAM, Lancashire: [li̲dh-əm], to rhyme with *with 'em* (i.e. *with them*). NOT [lɛidh-əm], rhyming with *try them*.

LYVEDEN, peer's title: [li̲v-dən], first syllable the same as *live*, verb. NOT [lɛi̲v-dən], first syllable the same as *live*, adjective.

MACABRE: [mə-ka̲hbr], two syllables. NOT [mə-ka̲h-bə], second syllable the same as *car*, or [mə-ka̲y-bə], second syllable rhyming with *say*, three syllables, though, surprisingly, both these last do exist.

MACAO: [mə-ko̲u], accent on second syllable, which is the same as *cow*.

MACATEER, Irish surname: [mak-ə-te̲e̲ə̲], to rhyme with *racketeer*. NOT [mə-ka̲t-eeə], accent on second syllable.

122

MACBEATH, Scotch surname: [mak-beth], the same as *Macbeth*.

MACCORQUODALE, Scotch surname: [mə-kawk-ə-dayl].

MACDONELL, Scotch surname: [mak-don-əl], accent on second syllable. But one family of the name calls it [mak-dən-el], accent on last syllable.

MACEVOY, Irish surname: [mak-ə-voi], accent on first syllable. NOT [mək-eev-oi], second syllable the same as *Eve*.

MACGILLYCUDDY. There are mountains in Ireland called *Macgillycuddy's Reeks* and an Irish personage called *The Macgillycuddy of the Reeks*: [mak-gli-kʌd-i], four syllables, accent on the third. NOT [mək-gil-i-kʌd-i], five syllables, accent on the second.

MACHIN, surname: [may-chin]. But the pronunciation [mach-in], first syllable the same as *match*, is also known.

MACHINATION: [mak-in-aysh-ən], first syllable the same as *mack*. NOT [mach-in-aysh-ən], first syllable the same as *match*, or [mash-in-aysh-ən], first syllable the same as *mash*.

MACHYNLLETH, Wales: [mə-hʌnth-leth].

MACINTYRE, Scotch surname: [mak-in-tah], or [mak-in-tɛiə], accent on first syllable. NOT [mə-kin-tah], or [mə-kin-tɛiə], accent on second.

MACIVER, Scotch surname: [mak-eev-ə], second syllable the same as *Eve*. But, in England, it is sometimes pronounced [mak-ɛiv-ə], second syllable the same as *I've*.

MACKAY, Scotch surname: [mə-kɛi], second syllable to rhyme with *guy*. NOT [mak-i], to rhyme with *Jacky*.

MACKEOWN, Irish surname: [mə-kee̯-yən], to rhyme with *Achæan*.

MACKIE, Scotch surname: [mak-i], to rhyme with *Jacky*.

MACLEAN, Scotch surname: [mə-klayn], second syllable to rhyme with *sane*. NOT [mə-kleen], second syllable rhyming with *seen*. The advertising slogan for the toothpaste, *Have you Macleaned your teeth to-day?* thus disregards the correct pronunciation.

MACLEHOSE, Scotch surname: [mak-li-hohz], accent on first syllable. NOT [mak-əl-hohz], first part rhyming with *shackle*.

MACLEOD, Scotch surname: [mə-kloud], second syllable the same as *cloud*.

MACLOUGHLIN, Irish surname: [mə-klok-lin], second syllable the same as *clock*.

MACNAMARA, Irish surname: [mak-nə-mah-rə], accent on third syllable which rhymes with *far*.

MACQUARRIE, Scotch surname: [mə-kwo-ri], second part the same as *quarry*. NOT [mə-kwa-ri], second part to rhyme with *Harry*.

MADAM: [mad-əm]. In some women's shops I understand that the pronunciation [mod-əm], to rhyme with *Sodom*, is used, though I have never actually heard it.

MADELINE, Christian name: [mad-lin], two syllables. OR [mad-ə-lin], three.

MAGDALEN *College*, Oxford: [mawd-lin], the same as *maudlin*. *Magdalene* College, Cambridge, is pronounced in the same way. Both these colleges take their name from St. Mary Magdalene, but she is pronounced [mag-də-leen], as spelt. (The adjective *maudlin* and *Magdalene* are one and the same word; the meaning of the former derives from pictures in which the Magdalen—that is, St. Mary Magdalene—is shown weeping.)

MAGRATH, Irish surname: [mə-grah], second syllable to rhyme with *far*. NOT [mə-grath], second syllable rhyming with *hath*.

MAINWARING, surname: [man-ə-ring], no W, first syllable the same as *man*. NOT [mayn-weə-ring], accent on second syllable and as spelt.

MAJORCA: [mə-jawk-ə], as spelt. But the many English tourists have tended, rather affectedly, to introduce the pronunciation belonging to its Spanish name *Mallorca* as [mɛi-yaw-kə].

MALAGA, Spain: [mal-ə-gə], accent on first syllable. NOT [mə-lahg-ə], accent on second.

The MALL, London: [mal], to rhyme with *pal*. [mawl], to rhyme with *Paul* is, perhaps, old-fashioned.

MALT: [mawlt]. NOT [molt].

MALVERN: [mawl-vən], with L. [maw-vən], without L, is very old-fashioned U.

MANAUS, Brazil: [mə-nay-os], for it used to be spelt *Manaos*.

MANNEQUIN: [man-i-kin], third syllable the same as *kin*. NOT [man-i-kwin], third syllable the same as *quin* (i.e. *quintuplet*).

MANUFACTURE: [man-ə-fak-chə]. OR [man-yʊ-fak-chə].

125

MAORI: [mah-ri], to rhyme with *starry*. OR [mou-ri], to rhyme with *cowrie*. But neither of these is the Maori pronunciation of the name.

MARASCHINO: [ma-rəs-keen-oh], third syllable the same as *keen*. NOT [ma-rə-sheen-oh], third syllable the same as *sheen*.

MARGARINE: [mah-jə-reen]; hence the abbreviation [mahj] *marge*, the same as *Marge*, non-U shortening of *Marjorie*. The older pronunciation [mah-gə-reen], second syllable the same as first syllable of *galore*, is now hardly used.

MARIA, Christian name: [mə-rɛiə], last part to rhyme with *higher*. The Americans use something like the Spanish pronunciation: [mə-ree-yə], second syllable to rhyme with *tea*; this pronunciation is now often heard in English too.

MARIE, Christian name: [mə-ree], accent on second syllable. NOT [ma-ri], the same as *marry*, or [mɛə-ri], the same as *Mary*.

MARION, Christian name: [ma-ri-yən], first two syllables the same as *marry*. But [mɛə-ri-yən], first two syllables the same as *Mary*, is also known.

MARITAL: [mar-it-əl], accent on first syllable. NOT [mə-rɛit-əl], last part rhyming with *title*.

MARLBOROUGH: [mawl-bə-rə], first syllable the same as *maul*; but [mahl-bə-rə], first syllable the same as *marl*, is also heard.

MARTELL, surname: [mah-tel], accent on second syllable.

MARTINEAU, surname: [mah-ti-noh], accent on first syllable.

MARYBOROUGH, Ireland: [ma-ri-brə], first part the same as *marry*, last part the same as that of *Edinburgh*. NOT as spelt.

126

MARYLEBONE, London: [mạ-ri-bən], three syllables, first part the same as *marry*. NOT [mạl-i-bən], first syllable to rhyme with *pal*; or [mạ̱hl-i-bən], first syllable the same as *marl*; or as spelt.

MASCULINE: [mạhs-kyʋ-lin], first syllable to rhyme with *farce*. OR [mạs-kyʋ-lin], first syllable to rhyme with *gas*.

MASTIFF: [mạs-tif], first syllable to rhyme with *gas*. OR [mạhs-tif], first syllable to rhyme with *farce*.

MATHER, surname. Usually [mạdh-ə], to rhyme with *blather*.

MATHESON, surname: [mạth-i-sən], three syllables.

MAUREEN, Christian name: [mo-rẹẹn], accent on second syllable. NOT [mạw-reen], accent on first.

MEATH, Ireland: [meedh], to rhyme with *breathe*. NOT [meeth], rhyming with *heath*.

MEDICAMENT: [me-dịk-ə-ment], accent on second syllable. NOT [mẹd-ik-ə-ment], accent on first.

MEDICINE: [mẹd-sən], two syllables. NOT [mẹd-i-sən] or [mẹd-i-sin], three.

MEDIEVAL: [med-i-ẹẹ-vəl], four syllables. NOT [med-ẹẹ-vəl], three.

MEIKLEJOHN, Scotch surname: [mịk-əl-jon], first part to rhyme with *tickle*. NOT [mɛịk-əl-jon], first part the same as *Michael*.

MEKONG, river: [mẹẹ-kọng], the two syllables being equally stressed.

MELBOURNE: [mel-bən], accent on first syllable. But the Victorian peer's title was apparently pronounced [mel-booən], accent on second syllable.

MEMO, a business and Civil Service word: [mem-oh], first syllable to rhyme with *stem*. NOT [meem-oh], first syllable to rhyme with *steam*.

MENAGERIE: [mən-ahj-ə-ri], second syllable to rhyme with *barge*. OR [mən-aj-ə-ri], second syllable to rhyme with *badge*.

MENDELSSOHN, surname: [men-dəl-sʌn], accent on first syllable.

MENTONE = *Menton*, France: [men-toh-ni], accent on second syllable, last part the same as *Tony*.

MENZIES, Scotch surname: [ming-iz], to rhyme with *thing is* (as in *The thing is*—). But [men-ziz]—that is, as spelt—in Australia, where the name is well known as that of a Prime Minister. The name had the Middle Scots letter ȝ, called *yogh*, which was pronounced [y]. In many handwritings it looked like a zed and came to be considered as one—hence the modern spelling of the name—and the second pronunciation. (The origin of *ye*, pseudo-archaic for *the*—as in *Ye olde Englishe tea shoppe*—is similar. In Middle English the definite article had the letter *thorn*, pronounced [th]. In some hand-writings thorn came to be written identically with Y.)

MEREDITH, surname: [me-ri-dith], accent on first syllable, in England. But [mə-red-ith], accent on second syllable, in Wales. Since the name *is* Welsh, in which language it is spelt *Maredudd*, the latter way must be regarded as the more correct.

METALLURGY: [me-tal-əj-i], accent on second syllable. OR [met-əl-urj-i], accent on first.

MEYNELL, surname: [mɛn-əl], to rhyme with *kennel*.

MEYRICK, surname: [mɛ-rik], to rhyme with *Eric*.

MIAMI: [mi-yam-i]; but the American pronunciation is [mɛi-yam-i].

MICHIE, Scotch surname: [mik-i], the same as *Micky*, but with Scotch *ch* in *loch*. NOT [mich-i], first syllable rhyming with *rich*.

MICHIGAN: [mich-i-gən], first syllable to rhyme with *ditch*. But the American pronunciation is [mish-i-gən], first syllable to rhyme with *dish*.

MIDWIFERY: [mid-wif-ə-ri], second syllable the same as *whiff*.

MIGRATORY: [mɛig-rə-tə-ri], accent on first syllable. NOT [mɛig-rayt-ə-ri], accent on second.

MILAN: [mi-lan], accent on second syllable. The old pronunciation [mi-lən], accent on first syllable, has died out, but survives in *milliner*, originally a dealer in haberdashery from Milan.

MILLAIS, surname of the artist: [mi-lay], no S. NOT [mi-lays] or [mi-layz], with S.

MILNGAVIE, Scotland: [mil-gɛi].

MINIATURE: [min-ə-chə]. OR [min-yə-chə].

MINOAN: [mi-noh-wən]. OR [mɛi-noh-wən].

MISCHIEVOUS: [mis-chi-vəs], three syllables, accent on the first. NOT [mis-cheev-i-yəs], four syllables, accent on second.

129

MISSOURI: [mi-saw-ri], last part to rhyme with *story*, but the American pronunciation is [mi-zṳ-ri].

MOGUL: [mə-gʌl], accent on second syllable. NOT [moh-gəl], rhyming with *ogle*. But the latter pronunciation was used in a recent television series.

MOHUN, surname: [moon], the same as *moon*.

MOLECULE: [mol-i-kyool], first syllable to rhyme with *doll*. NOT [mohl-i-kyool], first syllable the same as *mole*.

MOLYNEUX, surname. Usually [mol-i-nyooks], with the X sounded. But sometimes [mol-i-nyoo], without X.

MONACO: [mon-ə-koh], accent on first syllable. OR [mon-ah-koh], accent on second.

MONCREIFF, MONCREIFFE, MONCRIEFF. These Scotch surnames are all pronounced [mon-kreef], accent on second syllable, which rhymes with *grief*.

MONMOUTH: [mʌn-məth], first syllable to rhyme with *bun*; but many say [mon-məth], first syllable to rhyme with *on*.

MONS, Belgium: [monz], to rhyme with *bronze*.

MONTANA, U.S.A.: [mon-tahn-ə], second syllable the same as *tarn*; but the American pronunciation is [mon-tan-ə], second syllable the same as *tan*.

MONTEVIDEO: [mon-ti-vid-ay-yoh], accent on fourth syllable. NOT [mon-ti-vid-i-yoh], accent on third.

MOOR: [maw], the same as *maw*. OR [mooə].

MORALE: [mə-rahl], second syllable to rhyme with *marl*. NOT [mə-ral], second syllable rhyming with *pal*.

MORAN, Irish surname: [maw-rən], the same as *moron*. NOT [mə-ran], accent on second syllable, which is the same as *ran*.

MORAY *Firth*: [mʌ-ri], the same as *Murray*.

MORON: [maw-ron], to rhyme with *boron*. NOT [mo-rən], to rhyme with *sporran*. In MORONIC [mə-ro-nik], the accent is on the second syllable.

MORRELL, surname. Usually [mə-rel], accent on second syllable.

MOSCOW: [mos-koh], second syllable to rhyme with *toe*; [mos-kou], second syllable the same as *cow*, is American.

MOWBRAY, surname: [moh-bri], first syllable the same as *mow*. NOT [mou-bri], first syllable rhyming with *cow*.

MUIR, surname: [myaw], to rhyme with *your*.

MULCAHY, Irish surname: [mʌl-ka-hi], accent on second syllable.

MYTH: [mith], to rhyme with *kith*; [mɛith] is now rarely heard.

NAAS, Ireland: [nays], to rhyme with *pace*.

NAISH, surname: [nash], to rhyme with *crash*.

NAIVE: [nah-yeev], two syllables, accent on second. NOT [nayv], the same as *nave*.

NASMYTH, surname: [nay-smith], first syllable the same as *neigh*. NOT [nas-mith], first syllable rhyming with *gas*.

131

NASSAU, Bahamas: [nas-aw], accent on first syllable. NOT [nə-saw], accent on second.

NATAL, South Africa: [nə-tal], accent on second syllable.

NECESSARILY: [nes-ə-se-ri-li], accent on first syllable. NOT [nes-e-sęə-ri-li], last part rhyming with *warily*; [nes-e-se-ri-li], accent on third syllable, last part to rhyme with *merrily*, is possible.

NEPAL: [nə-pawl], accent on second syllable, which is the same as *Paul*.

NEPHEW: [nev-yʋ], first syllable to rhyme with *rev*. NOT [nef-yʋ], first syllable rhyming with *chef*.

NEPOTISM: [nep-o-tizm], first syllable to rhyme with *step*. OR [neep-o-tizm], first syllable to rhyme with *steep*.

NEWCASTLE: [nyoo-kahs-əl], accent on first syllable, second syllable to rhyme with *farce*. NOT [nyoo-kas-əl], accent on second syllable, which rhymes with *gas*.

NEWFOUNDLAND: [nyoo-fənd-lənd], accent on first syllable. OR [nyoo-found-lənd], accent on second.

New ORLEANS: [awl-i-yənz], accent on first syllable. Americans, other than those who live in the place, say [aw-leenz], second syllable the same as *leans*.

NICOLA, Christian name: [nik-ol-ə], accent on first syllable. NOT [nik-ohl-ə], accent on second.

NICOSIA, Cyprus: [nik-o-seeə], accent on third syllable. NOT [ni-koh-syə], accent on second.

132

NIHILIST: [nɛi-hil-ist], with H; [nɛi-yil-ist], without H, is perhaps rather old-fashioned.

NOMENCLATURE: [no-mɛn-klə-chaw], accent on second syllable. [noh-men-klə-chaw], accent on first syllable, is now disused.

NONCHALANT: [nọn-shə-lənt]. NOT [nọn-chə-lənt].

NONE: [nʌn], to rhyme with *dun*, but, in the Midlands, [non], to rhyme with *don*. The prefix *non-* (as in *non-starter*) is of course pronounced in the latter way. This causes confusion to the illiterate, so that they think *non-* is written *none*—*No access to none-frontagers!* (a notice seen in Birmingham).

NOOK: [nʊk]. NOT [nook].

NOREEN, Christian name: [no-rẹẹn], accent on second syllable. NOT [nạw-reen], accent on first.

NORTHANGER *Abbey*. The name is not a real one and no one knows how Jane Austen pronounced it, nor is there any tradition about this. Clearly, there are many ways in which it could be pronounced: (A) with extra H, so that the last part is the same as *hangar*; or (B) without H and, then, last two syllables to rhyme with *banger* (or with this plus inserted G—[bang-gə]), or second syllable to rhyme with either *flange* or *grange*. Accent on either first or second syllable. The most favoured pronunciation is [nạwth-ang-gə]. The other possibilities are: [nạwth-hang-ə], [nawth-hạng-ə], [nạwth-ang-ə], [nawth-ạng-ə], [nawth-ạng-gə], [nạwth-an-je], [nawth-ạn-jə], [nạwth-ayn-jə], [nawth-ạyn-jə]. In Charlotte Brontë's juvenile work *Legends of Angria*, there is an Alexander Percy, Earl of Northangerland. This name did not derive from Jane Austen, nor, in all probability is it from *Ingermanland* (near Leningrad), for which one of the Russian names is *Ingriya* (which

133

is rather like *Angria*). *Northangerland* is probably *Northumber-land* mixed up with the ordinary word *anger*.

NORTHOLT, airfield: [na̲wth-hohlt], with extra H.

NORWICH: [no̲r-ij], to rhyme with *porridge*. OR [no̲r-ich], second syllable to rhyme with *rich*.

NUNEATON: [nʌn-e̲e̲t-ən], accent on second syllable, first to rhyme with *dun*.

OBDURATE: [o̲b-dyʊ-rit], accent on first syllable. NOT [ob-dya̲w-rayt], accent on second.

OBLIGATORY: [ob-li̲g-ə-tri], four syllables, accent on second. NOT [ob-lig-a̲yt-ə-ri], five syllables, accent on third.

OBLIGED: [ob-le̲ijd]; the old U-pronunciation [ob-le̲e̲jd], second syllable to rhyme with that of *besieged*, was probably dead by 1900. It—and *tea* [tay], to rhyme with *pay*—are virtually the only two pronunciations made use of by popular novelists to indicate period talk.

OBOE: [o̲h-boh], second syllable to rhyme with *doe*. The pronunciation [o̲h-boi], second syllable the same as *boy*, is now hardly ever heard.

ODIOUS: [o̲h-dyəs]. The old U-pronunciation [o̲h-jəs] hardly survives.

OENONE, Christian name: [i-no̲h-ni].

OFF: [awf], to rhyme with *wharf*. OR [of], to rhyme with *doff*.

OFTEN: [aw-fən], no T, the same as *orphan*; or [of-ən], no T, first syllable to rhyme with *doff*. NOT [of-tən], with T.

OMDURMAN, Sudan: [om-də-man], accent on first syllable. NOT [om-dur-man], accent on second.

O'MEARA, Irish surname: [oh-mah-rə], second syllable to rhyme with *tar*.

OMINOUS: [om-in-əs], first syllable to rhyme with *Tom*. NOT [ohm-in-əs], first syllable to rhyme with *tome*. This latter pronunciation is due to association with *omen* [ohm-ən].

OMNISCIENCE: [om-nis-yəns], second syllable to rhyme with *hiss*. NOT [om-nish-yəns], second syllable rhyming with *wish*.

O'MORCHOE, Irish surname: [oh-mʌ-rə], last part to rhyme with *borough*.

ONIONS, surname. Usually the same as *onions*. But it has been pronounced [ə-nɛi-yənz], accent on second syllable, which is the same as *nigh*, to distinguish it from the ordinary word *onions*, which has comic overtones.

OONAGH, Irish Christian name: [oon-ə], to rhyme with *lunar*.

OPHTHALMIC. The only possible pronunciation seems to be the 'incorrect' one [op-thal-mik], first syllable to rhyme with *top*, instead of the correct [of-thal-mik], first syllable to rhyme with *doff*. Similarly OPHTHALMIA.

OPPOSITE: [op-ə-zit], last syllable to rhyme with *bit*. NOT [op-ə-sɛit] or [op-ə-zɛit], last syllable rhyming with *bite*.

OPUS: [op-əs], first syllable to rhyme with *pop*. OR [ohp-əs], first syllable to rhyme with *pope*.

ORANG-OUTANG: [ə-rang-ə-tang], accent on last syllable. The pronunciation [oh-rang-oo-tang], the first and third syllables being equally stressed, is pedantic, although it does resemble the Malay original of the word, which is *orang hutan* meaning 'man of the forest'.

ORDEAL: [aw-deeəl]. NOT [aw-deel], second syllable the same as *deal*.

ORDINARY: [aw-din-ri], three syllables. NOT [aw-din-eə-ri], four, the first and third being equally stressed.

ORGY: [aw-ji], to rhyme with *Georgie*. NOT [aw-gi], rhyming with *corgi*.

O'RIORDAN, Irish surname: [oh-raw-dən], last part to rhyme with *broaden*. NOT [oh-reiə-dən], middle part rhyming with *higher*; or [oh-reeə-dən], second syllable the same as *rear*.

O'SHAUGHNESSY, Irish surname: [oh-shaw-nes-i], accent on second syllable. No GH. NOT [oh-shaw-nes-i], accent on third.

O'SHEA, Irish surname: [oh-shay], second syllable to rhyme with *say*. NOT [oh-shee], second syllable the same as *she*.

OTAGO, New Zealand: [oh-tah-goh], second syllable the same as *tar*. NOT [ə-tay-goh], second syllable the same as *Tay*.

OUGHTRED, surname: [out-red], first syllable the same as *out*. NOT [awt-red], first syllable the same as *ought*, or [oot-red], first syllable rhyming with *boot*.

OUIDA, pseudonym of the novelist: [wee-də], two syllables, to rhyme with *feeder*.

136

OZONE: Chemists say [o̱h-zohn], accent on first syllable. The general public used to say [o-zo̱hn], accent on second syllable. Perhaps they still do.

PADUA: [pa̱d-yʊ-wə]. NOT [pa̱d-ʊ-wə].

PAKENHAM, surname: [pa̱k-ə-nəm], first syllable the same as *pack*. NOT [pa̱yk-ə-nəm], first syllable rhyming with *bake*.

PALL—noun (as in *a pall of smoke*) and verb (as in *it's beginning to pall on me*): [pawl], the same as *Paul*. NOT [pal], the same as *pal*.

PALLISER, surname: [pa̱l-is-ə], first syllable the same as *pal*. NOT [pa̱wl-is-ə], first syllable the same as *Paul*.

PALL MALL, London: [pe̱l me̱l], both syllables to rhyme with *hell*. The two syllables are equally stressed. OR [pa̱l ma̱l], both syllables to rhyme with *Hal*. NOT [pa̱wl ma̱wl], both syllables rhyming with *haul*.

PALTRY: [pa̱wl-tri], first syllable the same as *Paul*. NOT [po̱l-tri], first syllable rhyming with *doll*, or [pa̱l-tri], first syllable the same as *pal*.

PAMELA, Christian name: [pa̱m-əl-ə], accent on first syllable. [pəm-e̱el-ə], accent on the second, was apparently known in the eighteenth century but is now dead.

PANAMA: [pan-ə-ma̱h], accent on last syllable. But the American pronunciation is [pa̱n-ə-mah], accent on first.

PAPUA: [pa̱p-yʊ-ə], accent on first syllable. OR [pə-po̱o-wə], accent on second.

137

PARAFFIN: [par̪-ə-feen], last syllable to rhyme with *seen*. OR [par̪-ə-fin], last syllable to rhyme with *sin*.

PARAGRAPH: [par̪-ə-grahf], last syllable to rhyme with *scarf*. NOT [par̪-ə-graf], last syllable rhyming with *gaff*.

PARAGUAY: [par-ə-gwa̱y], last syllable to rhyme with *day*. OR [par-ə-gwɛ̱i̱], last syllable to rhyme with *die*. Accent on last syllable.

PARIAH: [par̪-i-yə], accent on first syllable. NOT [pə-rɛi-yə], rhyming with *Maria*.

PARLIAMENT: [pa̱ẖ-lə-mənt]. NOT [pa̱ẖ-lyə-mənt].

PARNELL, surname: [pah-nɛ̱l], accent on second syllable.

PARQUET: [pa̱ẖ-kay], second syllable to rhyme with *bay*. [pa̱ẖ-kit], second syllable the same as *kit*, is old-fashioned.

PARTICULAR: [pə-ti̱k-yʊ-lə], first syllable the same as that of *Peru*. NOT [pah-ti̱k-yʊ-lə], first syllable the same as *par*.

PASCALL, surname: [pa̱s-kəl], accent on first syllable. This name can be spelt *Pascal* (which is also the name of the philosopher), pronounced [pas-ka̱ẖl], accent on second syllable, which is the same as *Carl*.

PASS: [pahs], to rhyme with *farce*. NOT [pas], rhyming with *gas*.

PASSCHENDAELE, Belgium, known from 1914–18 War: [pa̱sh-ən-dayl], first two syllables the same as *passion*, last the same as *dale*.

PASTIME: [pa̱ẖs-tɛim], first syllable to rhyme with *farce*. NOT [pa̱s-tɛim], first syllable rhyming with *gas*.

138

PASTON, surname, well known from *The Paston Letters*—that fascinating and invaluable fifteenth-century collection. In this context the name is usually pronounced [pahs-tən], first syllable to rhyme with *farce*.

PASTY (e.g. *Cornish pasty*): [pas-ti], first syllable to rhyme with *gas*. NOT [pahs-ti], first syllable rhyming with *farce*.

PATENT, noun (of an invention) and adjective (as in *a patent fact* meaning 'a fact clear for all to see'). There are two pronunciations, [pat-ənt], first syllable the same as *pat*, and [payt-ənt], first syllable the same as *pate*. In official use the noun is pronounced in the first way. Usually the adjective is pronounced in the second way. *Patent leather*, which, since the word here refers to the fact that the thing was once patented, might well be pronounced in the first way, is almost invariably pronounced in the second.

PATH: [pahth], to rhyme with *hearth*. NOT [path], to rhyme with *hath*.

PATHAN—the people of this name live in Afghanistan (they were particularly well known in the days of the 'North-West Frontier'): [pə-tahn], accent on second syllable. NOT [pay-thən], rhyming with *Nathan*.

PATHOS: [payth-os], first syllable to rhyme with *faith*. NOT [path-os], first syllable rhyming with *hath*.

PATRIOT: [pat-ri-yət], first syllable to rhyme with *rat*. OR [payt-ri-yət], first syllable to rhyme with *rate*.

PAVIA, Italy: [payv-yə], the same as *paviour*. OR the Italian pronunciation.

PEARSALL, surname: [peeə-səl], first syllable the same as *peer*. NOT [peə-səl], first syllable the same as *pear*.

PEJORATIVE: [pẹej-ər-it-iv], accent on first syllable. OR [pə-jọr-ət-iv], accent on second.

PEKINESE, kind of dog: [pẹk-i-neez], first syllable the same as *peck*. OR [pẹek-i-neez], first syllable the same as *peak*.

PEKING = *Peiping*: [pee-kịng], as spelt. The older Europeanised form was *Pekin* [pee-kịn].

PEMBROKE: [pẹm-brʊk], second syllable the same as *brook*. NOT [pẹm-brohk], second syllable the same as *broke*.

PENNECUIK, Scotch surname: sometimes [pẹn-i-kʊk], last syllable the same as *cook*; sometimes [pẹn-i-kwik], last syllable the same as *quick*.

PENNEFATHER, surname: [pẹn-i-fedh-ə], accent on first syllable, last part the same as *feather*. NOT [pẹn-i-fahdh-ə], last part as spelt.

PENZANCE: [pen-zạns], second syllable to rhyme with *manse*. Accent on second syllable. NOT [pen-zạhns], second syllable rhyming with *France*.

PEPYS, surname. The diarist is normally called [peeps], the same as *peeps*. But present-day bearers of the surname usually call it [pẹp-iz], two syllables, first the same as *pep*.

PEREMPTORY: [pə-rẹm-tə-ri], accent on second syllable. NOT [pẹ-rem-ter-i], accent on first.

PERHAM, surname: [pẹ-rəm], no H. NOT [pụr-ham].

PERHAPS: [praps], one syllable, to rhyme with *flaps*. OR [pə-rạps], two syllables, without H. [pə-hạps], with H, is essentially a female pronunciation.

PERSEVERANCE: [pur-sə-veeə-rəns], accent on third syllable. NOT [pə-sev-ə-rəns], accent on second.

PERSIA: [pursh-ə]. OR [purzh-ə].

PESHAWAR: [pə-shou-wə], last part the same as *shower*.

PESTLE: [pes-əl], to rhyme with *nestle*. NOT [pest-əl], rhyming with *festal*.

PETRARCH, the poet. Usually [pet-rahk], first syllable the same as *pet*. But sometimes [peet-rahk], first syllable the same as *peat*.

PETRE, peer's title: [pee-tə], the same as *Peter*. NOT [pet-ri], two syllables, first the same as *pet*.

PETULA, Christian name: [pet-yʊ-lə], accent on first syllable. NOT [pə-tyoo-lə], accent on second.

PHARMACEUTICAL: [fah-mə-syoo-tik-əl], C as [s]. NOT [fah-mə-kyoo-tik-əl], C as [k].

PHELIM, Irish Christian name: [feel-im], first syllable the same as *feel*. NOT [fel-im], first syllable the same as *fell*.

PHILIPPINES: [fil-i-pɛinz], last syllable to rhyme with *signs*. OR [fil-i-peenz], last syllable to rhyme with *scenes*.

PHILOLOGY: [fil-ol-ə-ji], first syllable the same as *fill*. [fɛil-ol-ə-ji], first syllable the same as *file*, was at one time considerably used.

PHOENICIA: [fə-neesh-yə], second syllable to rhyme with *leash*. OR [fə-nish-yə], second syllable to rhyme with *dish*.

141

PHOTOGRAPH: [foh-tə-graf], last syllable to rhyme with *gaff*. OR [foh-tə-grahf], last syllable to rhyme with *scarf*.

PHRASEOLOGY: [frayz-i-yol-ə-ji], five syllables. NOT [frayz-ol-ə-ji], four.

PIANIST: [pyan-ist], two syllables. OR [pee-yə-nist], three.

PICTURE: [pik-chə], [kch] as *ckch* in *deck-chair*. NOT [pik-shə], [ksh] as *cks* in *cocksure*.

PIEDMONT, Italy: [peed-mont], first syllable to rhyme with *feed*.

PINCERS: [pins-əz], first syllable to rhyme with *mince*. But many people say [pinch-əz], first syllable to rhyme with *inch*, because they connect the word with *pinch*.

PIQUANT. The older pronunciation is [pee-kənt], to rhyme with *secant*. But many people say [pi-kant], or the Frenchified [pi-kont], accent on second syllable.

PIQUET: [pi-ket], accent on second syllable, with T. NOT [pee-kay], accent on first syllable, no T.

PIRACY: [pi-rə-si], to rhyme with last part of *conspiracy*. OR [pei-rə-si], first syllable the same as *pie*.

PISTACHIO: [pis-tahsh-i-yoh], second syllable to rhyme with *marsh*. NOT [pis-tahch-i-yoh], second syllable rhyming with *march*.

PITCAIRN *Island*. The local pronunciation is [pit-kurn], second syllable to rhyme with *burn*.

PLAID: [plad], to rhyme with *mad*. NOT [playd], rhyming with *made*.

142

PLAQUE: [plak], to rhyme with *hack*. [plahk], to rhyme with *heark*, is affected.

PLASTIC: [plas-tik], first syllable to rhyme with *gas*. NOT [plahs-tik], first syllable rhyming with *farce*.

PLATEAU: [plat-oh], accent on first syllable. [plat-oh], accent on second, is also possible.

PLEBISCITE: [pleb-is-it], three syllables, accent on first. NOT [pleb-i-seit-i], four syllables, accent on third, last part rhyming with *flighty*.

PLURAL: [plaw-rəl], to rhyme with *oral*. [plooə-rəl], first part to rhyme with some people's pronunciation of *poor*, is also used.

POETRY: [poh-wə-tri], three syllables, first to rhyme with *go*. OR [poi-tri], two syllables, first to rhyme with *boy*.

POITIERS, France: [poi-teeəz], accent on second syllable, which rhymes with *cheers*. OR the French pronunciation.

POLKA: [pol-kə], first syllable to rhyme with *doll*. OR [pohl-kə], first syllable the same as *pole*.

POLYMERISATION: [pə-lim-ə-rɛiz-aysh-ən], accent on fifth syllable. NOT [pol-i-mur-rɛiz-aysh-ən], accent on third syllable, which rhymes with *her*. This curious pronunciation has been heard.

POMEGRANATE: [pom-gran-it], three syllables. NOT [pom-ə-gran-it], four.

POMMEL: [pʌm-əl], first syllable to rhyme with *rum*. NOT [pom-əl], first syllable rhyming with *Tom*.

PONSONBY, surname: [pʌn-sən-bi], first syllable the same as *pun*. NOT as spelt.

PONTEFRACT, Yorkshire. The old pronunciation [pʌm-frit], two syllables, first to rhyme with *rum*, second with *bit*, has died out (except possibly in *Pontefract cakes*?), and the name is pronounced as spelt.

PONTYPRIDD: [pont-i-preedh], last syllable to rhyme with *breathe*. NOT [pont-i-pridh], last syllable rhyming with *with*.

POOR: [paw], the same as *paw*. OR [pooə].

PORPOISE: [paw-pəs], second syllable the same as that of *purpose*. NOT [paw-poiz], second syllable rhyming with *boys*.

Port SAID: [sayd], to rhyme with *shade*. NOT [sɛid], the same as *side*.

POULETT, peer's title: [pʊl-it], the same as *pullet*. NOT [poʊl-it], first syllable rhyming with *howl*; or [pool-it], first syllable the same as *pool*.

POWELL, Welsh surname. This is pronounced [poh-wəl], two syllables, first to rhyme with *go*, or even [pohl], one syllable, the same as *pole*. [poʊ-wəl], to rhyme with *trowel*, is felt to be more Welsh and correct. But the Welsh form is *Pwyll*.

POWYS, Wales: [poh-wis], first syllable to rhyme with *go*. NOT [poʊ-wis], first syllable rhyming with *cow*.

PRAGUE: [prahg]. The older pronunciation [prayg] existed until the 'thirties, for there was the 'joke'—in poor taste even then —*Don't be vague, ask for Prague*, in which *Prague* replaced *Haig* in the well-known whisky slogan. It was supposed to be said to Hitler before the occupation of Czecho-Slovakia.

144

PRALINE, a sweet made of almonds: [pra̲wl-een], first syllable to rhyme with *call*. OR [pra̲hl-een], first syllable to rhyme with *Carl*.

PREFERABLY: [pre̲f-rə-bli], three syllables, accent on first. NOT [prə-fu̲r-rə-bli], four syllables, accent on second.

PREMATURE: [pre̲m-ə-tyaw], first syllable to rhyme with *gem*. OR [pre̲e̲m-ə-tyaw], first syllable to rhyme with *beam*.

PREMIER: [pre̲m-yə], first syllable to rhyme with *gem*. NOT [pre̲e̲m-yə], first syllable rhyming with *beam*.

PREVOST, surname: [pre̲v-oh], no ST, accent on first syllable.

PRIDEAUX, surname: [pri̲d-oh], to rhyme with *widow*.

PRISTINE: [pri̲s-tin], second syllable to rhyme with *sin*; or [pri̲s-tεin], second syllable to rhyme with *sign*. Accent on first syllable. NOT [pri̲s-teen], second syllable rhyming with *seen*.

PRITCHARD, Welsh surname. In Wales usually [pri̲ch-əd], to rhyme with *Richard*. But many Englishmen say [pri̲ch-ahd], second syllable to rhyme with *hard*.

PRIVACY: [pri̲v-ə-si], first syllable to rhyme with *live*, verb. OR [prε̲iv-ə-si], first syllable to rhyme with *live*, adjective.

PROCESS: [pro̲hs-es], first syllable to rhyme with *dose*. The American pronunciation [pro̲s-es], first syllable to rhyme with *dross*, can also be heard.

PROJECTILE: [pro̲j-ək-tεil], accent on first syllable. [proj-e̲k-til], accent on second, third the same as *till*, is no longer used.

PROTAGONIST: [prot-a̲g-ə-nist], first syllable to rhyme with *cot*. OR [proht-a̲g-ə-nist], first syllable to rhyme with *coat*.

PROVOST: [prǫv-əst], with ST. But the officer of the Military Police is called to-day a [prǫv-oh], accent on first syllable, though formerly a [prov-ǫh], accent on the second—no ST.

PROWESS: [prǫu-wes], first syllable to rhyme with *how*. OR [prǫh-wes], first syllable to rhyme with *hoe*.

PSYCHOLOGY: [sɛi-kǫl-ə-ji], no P. [psɛi-kǫl-ə-ji], with P, is old-fashioned.

PUERTO RICO: The normal English form is *Porto Rico*, [pǎw-toh rẹẹ-koh].

PURPORT, verb: [pə-pǎwt], accent on second syllable. NOT [pǔr-pawt], accent on first—but this latter is the pronunciation of the noun.

PWLLHELI, Wales: [pʊl-thẹli].

PYTCHLEY, Northamptonshire: [pɛịch-li]. NOT [pịch-li], first syllable the same as *pitch*.

QUADRUPLE: [kwǫd-rʊ-pəl], accent on first syllable. OR [kwod-rǫǫp-əl], accent on second.

QUAFF: [kwof], to rhyme with *doff*; or [kwahf], to rhyme with *scarf*. NOT [kwaf], rhyming with *gaff*.

QUAGMIRE: First syllable [kwag], to rhyme with *bag*. OR [kwog], to rhyme with *bog*.

QUALM: [kwahm], to rhyme with *harm*. OR [kwawm], to rhyme with *warm*.

QUANDARY: [kwǫn-də-ri], accent on first syllable. NOT [kwon-dɛ̣ə-ri], accent on second.

146

QUANT, surname: [kwont], to rhyme with *want*. NOT [kwant], rhyming with *ant*, or [kwahnt], rhyming with *aunt*.

QUASI-: [kwa̱yz-i], to rhyme with *crazy*. There are eleven other ways in which the word is often pronounced. The vowel of the first syllable may be [a] in *pat*, or [ah] in *part*, or [ay] in *day*; the middle consonant may be [s] in *sin* or [z] in *zeal*. The first syllable may thus rhyme with *gas, has, farce, bars, pace* or *pays*; the second syllable may be [i] in *pit* or [ɛi] in *bite*. The eleven ways are thus:—[kwa̱s-i], [kwa̱z-i], [kwa̱hs-i], [kwa̱hz-i], [kwa̱ys-i], [kwa̱s-ɛi], [kwa̱z-ɛi], [kwa̱hs-ɛi], [kwa̱hz-ɛi], [kwa̱ys-ɛi], [kwa̱yz-ɛi].

QUENNELL, surname: [kwən-e̱l], accent on second syllable.

QUESTIONNAIRE: [kwes-chə-ne̱ə]. The pronunciation [kes-chə-ne̱ə], with [k], now sounds slightly pedantic.

QUIET: [kwaht], one syllable, to rhyme with *heart*. OR [kwɛiət], to rhyme with *diet*.

Don QUIXOTE: [kwi̱k-sət]. To use the Spanish pronunciation is affected.

QUOIT: [koit]. NOT [kwoit].

QUOTH, a pseudo-archaism meaning 'said': [kwohth], to rhyme with *both*. [kwoth], to rhyme with *moth*, has been used.

RAEBURN, surname: [ra̱y-bən], first syllable the same as *ray*.

RALEIGH, surname: [ra̱wl-i], to rhyme with *surely* is considered the 'best' pronunciation. But both [ra̱yl-i], to rhyme with *daily*, and [ra̱l-i], the same as *rally*, are in fact often used.

RALPH: [rayf], to rhyme with *safe*. But many say [ralf], to rhyme with *Alf*.

RANELAGH *Gardens*, London: [ran-ə-lə].

RANFURLY, peer's title: [ran-fə-li], accent on first syllable. NOT [ran-fur-li], accent on second.

RASPBERRY: [rahz-bər-i], no P, first syllable to rhyme with *cars*. NOT [rasp-bər-i], with P.

RATION: [rash-ən], to rhyme with *passion*, is normal to-day. This pronunciation came in during the 1914–18 War from the Army, which pronounced the word thus at a period when other people said [raysh-ən], to rhyme with *station*. This latter pronunciation can hardly be heard to-day.

RAWALPINDI, Pakistan: [raw-əl-pin-di], first syllable the same as *raw*.

REALLY: [reeə-li], first syllable the same as *rear*. NOT [ree-li], rhyming with *mealie*.

REAY, peer's title: [ray], the same as *ray*.

RECOGNISE: [rek-əg-nɛiz], accent on first syllable. [rek-ə-nɛiz], without G, is often heard in hasty—sometimes called 'slovenly'—speech. NOT [rek-əg-nɛiz], accent on third syllable.

RECONDITE: [rek-ən-dɛit], accent on first syllable, third syllable to rhyme with *bite*. OR [rə-kʌn-dit], accent on second syllable, last part to rhyme with *pundit*; or [rə-kʌn-dɛit].

REFECTORY: [rə-fɛk-tri], accent on second syllable, to students; but [ref-ik-tri], accent on first, to many monks.

148

REFUGE: [ref-yooj], second syllable to rhyme with *stooge*. NOT [ref-yoozh], second syllable to rhyme with *rouge*.

REIMS: [reemz], to rhyme with *dreams*. To use the French pronunciation would be affected.

RELATIVIST, mathematician who specialises in Relativity: [rə-lat-ə-vist], accent on second syllable. NOT [rel-ə-tiv-ist], accent on first.

RELAY, noun. Of a race, [ree-lay], accent on first syllable. But in some other meanings [rə-lay], accent on second.

RENEGUE (also spelt RENEGE): [rə-nayg], second syllable to rhyme with *vague*. NOT [rə-neeg], second syllable rhyming with *league*, or [rə-nej], second syllable rhyming with *edge*.

RENNELL, surname: [ren-əl], accent on first syllable. NOT [rə-nel], accent on second.

RENWICK, surname: [ren-ik], no W.

REPUTABLE: [rep-yʊ-tə-bəl], accent on first syllable. NOT [rə-pyoo-tə-bəl], accent on second.

RESEARCH: [rə-surch], accent on second syllable. But the American pronunciation [ree-surch], accent on the first syllable, is much used.

RESOLVE: [rə-zolv]. NOT [rə-zohlv].

RESOURCEFUL: [rə-saws-fʊl], second syllable the same as *sauce*. But [rə-zaws-fʊl] is often heard.

RESPITE: [res-pit], accent on first syllable. NOT [rə-speit], accent on second.

RESTAURANT: French pronunciation, no final T. NOT [rest-ə-ront], last syllable rhyming with *want*.

RESTORATIVE, noun: [rə-sto-rə-tiv]. OR [rə-staw-rə-tiv], second syllable the same as *store*.

RETCH: [reech], the same as *reach*. OR [rech], the same as *wretch*.

REVEILLE: [rə-val-i], last part the same as *valley*. NOT [rə-vel-i], last part rhyming with *belly*.

REVERBERATORY: [rə-vurb-ə-tri], four syllables, accent on second. NOT [rə-vurb-ə-rayt-ə-ri], six syllables, accent on fourth.

REVOLT: [rə-vohlt], second syllable to rhyme with *jolt*. NOT [rə-volt].

RHODESIA: [roh-deesh-yə], second syllable to rhyme with *leash*. OR [roh-deezh-yə].

RHONDDA, Wales: [ron-də], to rhyme with *wander*.

RHYS, Welsh surname: [rees], to rhyme with *peace*. It is thus often spelt *Rees*. In Ireland, however, where *Rhys* is not uncommon, it is pronounced [reis], the same as *rice*.

RIBALD: [rib-əld], first syllable the same as *rib*. [reib-awld], first syllable to rhyme with *tribe*, is old-fashioned.

RIDEOUT, surname: [reid-out], first syllable the same as *ride*. NOT [rə-dout], the same as *redoubt*.

RIEVAULX *Abbey*, Yorkshire: [riv-əlz], to rhyme with *drivels*.

150

RIGA: [ree-gə], to rhyme with *eager*. But the pronunciation [rɛi-gə] was in use, because, in the well-known limerick, the word rhymes with *tiger*.

RIGEL, star-name: [rɛig-əl], first syllable to rhyme with that of *tiger*. NOT [reeg-əl], the same as *regal*; or [rig-əl], the same as *wriggle*.

RIGOR: [ri-gə], the same as *rigour*. OR [rɛi-gə], to rhyme with *tiger*.

RINTOUL, Scotch surname: [rin-tool], accent on second syllable. NOT [rin-tool], accent on first.

The RIVIERA: [riv-i-yɛə-rə], four syllables, last two to rhyme with *bearer*. NOT [riv-ee-rə], the same as *revere 'er* (i.e. *revere her*).

ROBESON, surname: Usually [rohb-sən], two syllables. The pronunciation [rob-i-sən], three syllables, is not common.

ROLFE, surname: [rohlf]. NOT [rolf].

ROMANCE: [roh-mans], second syllable the same as *manse*. NOT [roh-mahns], second syllable rhyming with *France*; or [roh-mans], accent on first syllable, which is American.

ROMANY: [rom-ə-ni], first syllable to rhyme with *Tom*. NOT [rohm-ən-i], first syllable rhyming with *tome*.

ROMNEY *Marsh*, Kent: [rʌm-ni], first syllable the same as *rum*, is perhaps better than [rom-ni], first syllable to rhyme with *Tom*.

ROMSEY, Hampshire: [rʌm-zi], first syllable the same as *rum*. NOT [rom-zi], first syllable rhyming with *Tom*.

151

ROOM: [rʊm]. OR [room], to rhyme with *doom*.

ROSYTH: [ros-ɛ̱ith], accent on second syllable.

ROTHES, Scotland: [ro̱th-iz], first syllable to rhyme with *moth*, second the same as -*es* in *houses*.

ROUGE: [roozh]. NOT [rooj], rhyming with *stooge*.

ROUGHTON, surname: [ro̱u-tən], first syllable to rhyme with *cow*. NOT [ra̱w-tən], first syllable rhyming with *caw*.

ROUMANIA. The name is pronounced [rʊ-ma̱yn-yə], last part the same as *mania*. This pronunciation is used even though the name is written *Romania* or *Rumania*.

ROUTE: [root], the same as *root*. But in the Army—*route march* —[rout], to rhyme with *stout*.

ROUTINE: [roo-te̱e̱n], accent on second syllable. But in phrases such as *routine check* the accent is often on the first, [ro̱o-teen].

ROUTLEDGE, surname: [rʌt-lij], first syllable the same as *rut*. NOT [ro̱ut-lij], first syllable the same as *rout*.

ROWAN: [ro̱h-wən], first syllable to rhyme with *hoe*. OR [ro̱u-wən], first syllable to rhyme with *how*.

ROWLEY, surname: [ro̱hl-i], to rhyme with *holy*. NOT [ro̱ul-i], rhyming with *Cowley*.

ROWLOCK: [rʌl-ək], first syllable to rhyme with *dull*. NOT [ro̱h-lok], as spelt.

ROXBURGH, Scotland: [ro̱ks-brə], first syllable as spelt, second the same as the end of *Edinburgh*.

RUBBISH: [rʌb-ish], as spelt. The pronunciation [rʌb-ij], second syllable to rhyme with *midge*, is dialectal.

RUCKSACK: [rʊk-sak], first syllable to rhyme with *look*; but the pronunciation [rʌk-sak], first syllable to rhyme with *luck*, is often heard.

RUE (verb): [roo], to rhyme with *do*; sometimes [ryoo], to rhyme with *dew*.

RUISLIP, Middlesex: [rᴇiz-lip], first syllable the same as *rise*.

RUSE: [rooz], to rhyme with *booze*. But [roos], to rhyme with *loose*, is often heard. Also [ryooz], to rhyme with *fuse*, and [ryoos], to rhyme with *deuce*.

RUTHIN, Wales: [rith-in], first syllable to rhyme with *pith*.

RUTHVEN, Scotch surname: [riv-ən], the same as *riven*.

RUTHWELL, village in Scotland where there is a celebrated Anglo-Saxon cross: [riv-əl], to rhyme with *drivel*. But anglo-saxonists mostly pronounce the name as spelt.

SABINE, surname: [sab-ɛin], accent on first syllable, which rhymes with *tab*. NOT [sə-bɛin], accent on second.

SACHEVERELL, surname: [sə-shev-ər-əl], accent on second syllable.

St. ASAPH, Wales: [as-əf], first syllable to rhyme with *gas*. NOT [ayz-əf], first syllable rhyming with *gaze*.

St. HELENA: [hə-leen-ə], accent on second syllable. NOT [hel-ə-nə], accent on first.

ST. JOHN, surname: [sin-jən], first syllable the same as *sin*, second the same as that of *dungeon*. NOT as spelt.

St. MORITZ, Switzerland: [mo-rits], accent on second syllable. OR [mor-its], accent on first.

ST. NEOTS, Huntingdonshire: [sənt-neets], second syllable to rhyme with *feats*. NOT [sənt-ni-yots], three syllables, as spelt. The pronunciation [snohts], one syllable, to rhyme with *boats*, is hardly heard to-day.

SALMON: [sam-ən], to rhyme with *Mammon*. NOT [sal-mən], first syllable rhyming with *pal*, or [sahl-mən], first syllable rhyming with *marl*.

SALONICA, Greece, known from 1914–18 War: [sal-ə-neek-ə], accent on third syllable. OR [səl-on-ik-ə], accent on second.

SALT: [sawlt]. NOT [solt].

SALTOUN, peer's title: [sol-toon], accent on second syllable.

SALVE; verb (as in *to salve one's conscience*), or noun (as *lip-salve*): [salv], to rhyme with *valve*. The pronunciation [sahv], to rhyme with *carve*, no L, is rather old-fashioned.

SALVER: [sal-və], first syllable to rhyme with *pal*. OR [sawl-və], first syllable to rhyme with *Paul*.

SALZBURG, Austria: [salts-burg]. To use the German pronunciation would be slightly pedantic.

SAMOYED, kind of dog: [sam-o-yayd], third syllable to rhyme with *braid*. OR [sam-o-yed], third syllable to rhyme with *bread*; accent on first syllable. OR [sam-oi-yed], accent on second.

154

SAMPLE: [sa̲hm-pəl], first syllable the same as *psalm*. NOT [sa̲m-pəl], first syllable the same as *Sam*. Similarly SAMPLER.

SANDEMAN, surname: [sa̲n-di-man], three syllables, first two the same as *sandy*.

SAN SEBASTIÁN: [sa̲n seb-a̲st-yən], which is not the Spanish pronunciation.

SANSKRIT: [sa̲ns-krit], first syllable to rhyme with *manse*. NOT [sa̲hns-krit], first syllable rhyming with *France*.

SANTA CRUZ. The various places of this name are usually called [sa̲n-tə krᴧz], last syllable to rhyme with *buzz*. OR [sa̲n-tə kroͅoͅz], last syllable to rhyme with *booze*. The Spanish pronunciation differs from these two.

SARAH, Christian name. Usually [sɛ̯ə-rə], to rhyme with *bearer*. But sometimes [sa̲h-rə], to rhyme with last part of *tiara*.

SARAWAK: [sar-ə-wa̲k], accent on third syllable. OR [sə-ra̲h-wak], accent on second.

SAUCHIEHALL *Street*, Glasgow. First part to rhyme with *rocky*, but with Scotch *ch* in *loch*.

SAULT STE. MARIE, Canada: [soo-sənt-mɛ̯ə-ri], last part the same as *Mary*.

SAUNDERS, surname. Usually [sa̲hn-dəz], first syllable to rhyme with *barn*. But sometimes [sa̲wn-dəz], first syllable to rhyme with *born*.

SAYS: [sez], to rhyme with *fez*. NOT [sayz], rhyming with *phase*.

SCA FELL, Cumberland: [skaw-fe̲l], accent on second syllable, first the same as *score*.

155

SCALLOP and SCOLLOP are one and the same word. It has various meanings; thus, as a noun, it can mean 'a kind of shell-fish' or 'a kind of ornament sewn on a garment'. Some people choose one of the two spellings and use this for any meaning, others vary the spelling according to the meaning. The same is true of the pronunciation: some people say [skǫl-əp], to rhyme with *wallop*, whatever the spelling or meaning; others say [skạl-əp], to rhyme with *gallop*. Some pronounce the word according as to how they spell it; others reserve one particular pronunciation for one particular meaning. It seems to be a matter of personal idiosyncrasy.

SCHEDULE: [shẹd-yʊl], first syllable the same as *shed*. The American pronunciation is [skẹj-ool], first syllable to rhyme with *hedge*, second with *fool*.

SCHOLAR: [skǫl-ə]. The pronunciation [skǫl-əd], to rhyme with *Lollard*, with final D, is dialectal.

SCONE: [skon], to rhyme with *don*. NOT [skohn], rhyming with *moan*. But in the *Stone of Scone* it is [skoon], to rhyme with *soon*.

SCRIMGEOUR, surname: [skrịm-jə], second syllable the same as that of *injure*. NOT [skrịm-jaw], second syllable the same as *jaw*.

SCUDAMORE, surname: [skyǫo-də-maw], first syllable the same as *skew*. NOT [skʌd-ə-maw], first syllable the same as *scud*.

SEAFORD, Sussex: [sẹe-fawd], second syllable the same as *ford*. NOT [sẹe-fəd], second syllable the same as that of *Oxford*.

SEAN, Irish Christian name: [shawn], the same as *shorn*.

SEATTLE, U.S.A.: [see-yạt-əl], accent on second syllable, last part to rhyme with *battle*.

SECOMBE, surname. Usually [seek-əm], first syllable the same as *seek*. But sometimes [sek-əm], first syllable to rhyme with *deck*.

SECOND, verb: [sə-kond], accent on second syllable, which rhymes with *fond*, when it means 'transfer' (military, etc.). Otherwise [sek-ənd], the same as the adjective.

SECRETARY: [sek-rə-tə-ri], four syllables; but [sek-ə-tri], three, is often heard.

SECRETIVE: [see-krə-tiv], accent on first syllable. OR [sə-kree-tiv], accent on second.

SEDBERGH, Yorkshire: [sed-bə], second syllable the same as last syllable of *November*.

SELSEY *Bill*: [sels-i], first syllable to rhyme with *else*. NOT [selz-i], first syllable the same as *sells*.

SEMINAL: [seem-in-əl], first syllable the same as *seem*. OR [sem-in-əl], first syllable to rhyme with *hem*.

SEMPILL, surname: [sem-pəl], to rhyme with *temple*.

SENEGAL: [sen-i-gawl], accent on last syllable, which rhymes with *Paul*. NOT [sen-i-gal], last syllable rhyming with *pal*; or [sen-i-gawl], [sen-i-gal], accent on first syllable.

SERBIA: [surb-yə], first syllable to rhyme with *blurb*. The pronunciation of the 1914–18 War was [surv-yə], first syllable the same as *serve*, with spelling *Servia*.

SEVASTOPOL', U.S.S.R. Known from the Crimean War as [se-bast-ə-pəl], with [b]. This pronunciation does not greatly resemble the Russian one.

SEVILLE. Normally [sə-vi̱l], accent on second syllable. But the oranges are called [se̱v-il], accent on the first.

SHEIKH: [sheek], to rhyme with *beak*. OR [shayk], the same as *shake*.

SHELLAC: [shə-la̱k], accent on second syllable. OR [she̱l-ak], accent on first.

SHREWSBURY: [shro̱hz-bər-i], first syllable to rhyme with *doze*. NOT [shro̱o̱z-bər-i], first syllable rhyming with *booze*.

SIDEBOTTOM, surname. Pronounced as spelt. The pronunciation [sid-i-bot-o̱hm], four syllables, accent on the last, first two to rhyme with *giddy*, may have been a joke, or may actually have existed.

SIERRA LEONE: [sye̱r-ə li-yo̱hn], no final E. NOT [sye̱r-ə-li-yo̱hn-i], with final E.

SIEVWRIGHT, surname: [si̱v-rɛit], first syllable to rhyme with *give*.

SIMULTANEOUS: [sim-əl-ta̱yn-yəs], first syllable to rhyme with *limb*. OR [sɛim-əl-ta̱yn-yəs], first syllable to rhyme with *lime*. So also SIMULTANEOUSLY, perhaps a word of more frequent use than *simultaneous*.

SINECURE: [si̱n-i-kyaw], first syllable the same as *sin*. OR [sɛi̱n-i-kyaw], first syllable the same as *sign*.

SINGAPORE: [sing-gə-pa̱w], accent on last syllable. OR [si̱ng-gə-paw], accent on first.

SIOUX: [soo], to rhyme with *moo*. No X. NOT [si̱-yoo], two syllables.

158

SKAGERRAK, strait between Norway and Denmark: [skah-gə-rak], first syllable the same as *scar*, the first and third syllables being equally stressed. OR [skag-ə-rak], accent on the first syllable, which rhymes with *bag*.

SKEGNESS: [skeg-nes], accent on second syllable.

SKI: [skee]. OR [shee], the same as *she*.

SKIDDAW, Cumberland: [skid-aw], accent on first syllable. OR [ski-daw], accent on second.

SLEIGHT: [slɛit], the same as *slight*. NOT [slayt], the same as *slate*.

SLOGAN: [slohg-ən], first syllable to rhyme with *vogue*. NOT [slog-ən], first syllable the same as *slog*.

SMETHWICK, Staffordshire: [smedh-ik], no W.

SMYTHE, surname: [smɛidh], to rhyme with *blithe*. But it is merely a spelling of *Smith*.

SNOOKER: [snook-ə]. NOT [snυk-ə].

SOFT: [sawft], to rhyme with *dwarfed*. OR [soft], to rhyme with *doffed*.

SOJOURN: [sʌj-ən], first syllable to rhyme with *budge*. NOT [soj-ən], first syllable rhyming with *lodge*.

SOLDER: [sod-ə], no L, first syllable to rhyme with *God*. NOT [sold-ə], first syllable rhyming with *lolled*; or [sohld-ə], first syllable the same as *sold*.

159

SOLIHULL, Warwickshire: [sol-i-hʌl], first syllable to rhyme with *doll*. OR [sohl-i-hʌl], first syllable to rhyme with *dole*. Accent on last syllable.

SOLVE: [solv]. NOT [sohlv].

SOMBRE: [som-bə], first syllable to rhyme with *Tom*. OR [sohm-bə], first syllable to rhyme with *tome*.

SOMERS, surname: [sʌm-əz], the same as *summers*.

SOMERVILLE, surname: [sʌm-ə-vil], first two syllables the same as *summer*.

SONOROUS: [sə-naw-rəs], accent on second syllable. NOT [son-ə-rəs], accent on first.

SOOT: [sʊt], to rhyme with *foot*. NOT [soot], rhyming with *boot*; or [sʌt], rhyming with *but*.

SOUGH: [sʌf], to rhyme with *puff*. [sou], to rhyme with *how*, and [soo], to rhyme with *who*, seem now to be obsolete.

SOUTHEY, surname. The poet is called [soudh-i], first syllable to rhyme with *mouth*, verb. NOT [sʌdh-i], first syllable the same as that of *southern*.

SOUTHWARK, London: [sʌdh-ək], first syllable the same as that of *southern*.

SPECIES: [spees-eez], first syllable to rhyme with *lease*. OR [speesh-eez], first syllable to rhyme with *leash*.

SPINACH: [spin-ij], second syllable to rhyme with *ridge*. NOT [spin-ich], second syllable rhyming with *rich*.

160

SPINET: [spin-et], accent on second syllable. NOT [spin-et], accent on first.

SPITSBERGEN: [spits-burg-ən], accent on second syllable. OR [spits-burg-ən], accent on first.

SPONGE-CAKE: [spʌnj-kayk], the two syllables being equally stressed. OR [spʌnj-kayk], accent on the first syllable only.

SPONTANEITY: [spon-tə-nee-yi-ti], third syllable the same as *knee*. NOT [spon-tə-nay-yi-ti], third syllable the same as *neigh*.

SPOON: [spoon], to rhyme with *moon*. NOT [spʊn].

SRINAGAR, India: [sər-i-nahg-ə], four syllables.

STANCE: [stahns], to rhyme with *France*. OR [stans], to rhyme with *manse*.

STANHOPE, surname: [stan-əp], no H.

STATUS *quo*: [stayt-əs], first syllable to rhyme with *rate*. OR [stat-əs], first syllable to rhyme with *rat*. But, in other uses (e.g. *status symbol*), the word has the first pronunciation.

STAUNCH: [stawnch], to rhyme with *paunch*. The pronunciation [stahnch], to rhyme with *branch*, is rather old-fashioned.

Old STEYNE, Brighton: [steen], to rhyme with *seen*. NOT [stein], rhyming with *sign*; or [stayn], rhyming with *sane*.

STEYNING, Sussex: [sten-ing], first syllable to rhyme with *pen*.

STIRRUP: [sti-rʌp]. The pronunciation [stʌ-rʌp] has been used by the U.

STRABANE, Ireland: [strə-bạn], second syllable the same as *ban*. Accent on second syllable. NOT [strə-bạyn], second syllable the same as *bane*.

STRACHAN, surname: [strạk-ən], to rhyme with *bracken*, but with Scotch *ch* in *loch*; outside Scotland the name is often pronounced [strawn], to rhyme with *born*.

STRATOSPHERE: [strạt-əs-feeə], first syllable to rhyme with *rat*. OR [strạyt-əs-feeə], first syllable to rhyme with *rate*.

STREATFIELD, surname: [strẹt-feeld], first syllable to rhyme with *bet*, second the same as *field*.

STRENGTH: [strength]. NOT [strenth], rhyming with *tenth*.

STROMBOLI, volcano in Italy: [strom-bọhl-i], accent on second syllable. OR [strọm-bol-i], accent on first.

STUPID: [styụp-id]. The pronunciations [stụp-id] and [stọop-id] were at one time U.

STURDEE, surname: [stụr-dẹe], the first and second syllables being equally stressed. NOT usually [stụr-di], the same as *sturdy*.

SUBMARINER, one who works in submarines. Navy: [sʌb-mạ-rin-ə], accent on second syllable—thus the last part the same as the word *mariner*. NOT [sʌb-mə-rẹe-nə], like *submarine*. The Naval pronunciation sounds like a joke, and may have originated as this.

SUBSIDENCE: [sʌb-sid-əns], accent on first syllable. But [səb-sẹid-əns], accent on second, is often heard.

SUBSTANTIAL: [sʌb-stạnsh-əl], second syllable to rhyme with first syllable of *mansion*. OR [sʌb-stạḥnsh-əl], second syllable to rhyme with *blanch*.

SUCCESSOR: [sək-sẹs-ə], accent on second syllable; [sʌk-ses-ə], accent on first syllable, is U-Catholic.

SUDAN: [sʊ-dạn], second syllable the same as *Dan*. OR [sʊ-dạḥn], second syllable the same as *darn*.

SUIT: [syoot], to rhyme with *cute*. The pronunciation [soot], to rhyme with *coot*, is a little old-fashioned.

SURE: [shaw], the same as *Shaw*. OR [shooə], to rhyme with many people's pronunciation of *poor*.

SURVEY, noun: [sụrv-ay], accent on first syllable. NOT [sə-vạy], accent on second—which is the pronunciation of the verb.

SUWANEE *River*, U.S.A.: [swọn-i], to rhyme with *bonny*—at least in the pseudo-negro song.

SWANSEA: [swọnz-i], first syllable to rhyme with *bronze*. NOT [swọns-i], first syllable rhyming with *nonce*.

SYRUP: [sị-rʌp]. NOT [sʌ-rʌp].

TACKLE, nautical: [tạyk-əl], first syllable the same as *take*; but [tạk-əl], to rhyme with *cackle*, in Fishing and Rugger.

TACTICS. Pronounced [tạ-tiks], without first C, to rhyme with *Statics*, by those who use the word professionally—especially in the Navy. (It is often opposed to *strategy*.) Others may pronounce the word [tạk-tiks], as spelt. Similarly TACTICAL, TACTICALLY.

163

TALCUM: [tạl-kəm], first syllable to rhyme with *pal*. NOT [tạwl-kəm], first syllable rhyming with *Paul*.

TAMPION, a piece of wood inserted into the muzzle of a gun. Pronounced [tọm-pyən], first syllable the same as *Tom*, in the Navy. NOT [tạm-pyən], rhyming with *champion*. The word is often spelt *tompion*, with O, but this spelling is false and due to the Naval pronunciation, for the word is connected with the verb *tamp*, with A, meaning 'to ram home an explosive charge'.

TARPAULIN: [tah-pạwl-in], accent on second syllable. OR [tạh-pə-lin], accent on first.

TATHAM surname: [tạyt-əm] to rhyme with *hate 'em* (i.e. *hate them*). OR [tạyth-əm], first syllable to rhyme with *faith*.

TEGUCIGALPA, Honduras: [te-goos-i-gạl-pə], accent on fourth syllable. Those who know the place often shorten its name to *Teguc* [te-gọọs].

TEIGNMOUTH, Devon: [tịn-məth], first syllable the same as *tin*. NOT [tạyn-məth], first syllable to rhyme with *rain*; or [tạyn-mouth], [tịn-mouth], second syllable the same as *mouth*.

TELEGRAPH: [tẹl-i-graf], last syllable to rhyme with *gaff*. OR [tẹl-i-grahf], last syllable to rhyme with *scarf*.

TEMPORARILY: [tẹmp-rə-ri-li], four syllables, accent on the first. NOT [temp-ə-rẹẹ-ri-li], or [temp-ə-rạ-ri-li], or [temp-ə-rạh-ri-li], five syllables, accent on the third.

TENET: [tẹn-it], to rhyme with *rennet*. But [tẹẹn-it], to rhyme with *seen it*, is often used.

TEVIOT, Scotland: [tẹẹv-yət], first syllable to rhyme with *reeve*. NOT [tẹv-yət], first syllable rhyming with *rev*.

164

TEYNHAM, peer's title: [tayn-əm], first syllable to rhyme with *sane*. NOT [teen-əm], first syllable rhyming with *seen*.

THAME, Oxfordshire: [taym], the same as *tame*.

THANK YOU!: [thengk-yʋ] or [thangk-yʋ], first syllable to rhyme with *bank*, second syllable the same as that of *nephew*. [thengk-yə], [thangk-yə], second syllable the same as the last syllable of *behaviour*, are old-fashioned U. [hengk-yʋ], [hangk-yʋ], H instead of TH, are often heard.

THEOBALDS *Road*, London. It is doubtful how far the old pronunciation [tib-əldz], first syllable to rhyme with *rib*, survives. Most people now pronounce the name as it is spelt.

THEODORIC, Christian name: [thi-yod-rik], accent on second syllable. NOT [thee-yod-rik], accent on first, or [thi-yo-dor-ik], four syllables, accent on third.

THRASH is often pronounced [thrash], to rhyme with *mash*; and THRESH is often pronounced [thresh], to rhyme with *mesh*. But the two get confused, so that [thrash-ing] *machine* and *to* [thresh] *the question out* have been heard.

THROGMORTON *Street*: [throg-mawt-ən], accent on second syllable.

TIERNEY, surname: [teeə-ni], accent on first syllable, which rhymes with *beer*.

TIGHE, surname: [tɛi], the same as *tie*.

TILDESLEY, surname: [tilz-li], no D.

TIMBRE: [tam-bə], to rhyme with *amber*. So it has been suggested that the word should be spelt *tamber*. But the French pronunciation is often used.

165

TINTAGEL, Cornwall: [tin-taj-əl], accent on second syllable.

TISSUE: [tis-yʊ], first syllable to rhyme with *hiss*. OR [tish-ʊ], first syllable to rhyme with *dish*.

TODHUNTER, surname: [tod-hʌn-tə], accent on second syllable.

TOKAY, wine (from *Tokaj*, Hungary): [tə-kay], second syllable to rhyme with *day*, which is not the Hungarian pronunciation. Also [tə-kɛi], second syllable to rhyme with *die*.

TOLEDO: [tə-leed-oh], second syllable the same as *lead* (verb). OR [tə-layd-oh], second syllable the same as *laid*.

TOLL, verb: [tohl], to rhyme with *dole*. NOT [tol], rhyming with *doll*.

TONBRIDGE, Kent: [tʌn-brij], the same as *Tunbridge* (*Wells*). NOT [ton-brij], first syllable rhyming with *don*.

TOOK: [tʊk]. NOT [took].

TOPGALLANT, kind of sail: [tə-gal-ənt], no P. The thing belongs to the period when sailing-ships were in use, but the pronunciation survives at least in the Navy, because Naval Cadets still learn about sails.

TORTOISE: [tawt-əs], the same as *taught us*—as indeed was appreciated by Lewis Carroll—'"We called him Tortoise because he taught us", said the Mock Turtle' (*Alice in Wonderland*, Chapter IX). NOT [taw-toiz], second syllable the same as *toys*.

TOSS: [tos], to rhyme with *Ross*. [taws], to rhyme with *force*, is very old-fashioned U.

TOURNAMENT. Normally [taw-nə-mənt], first syllable to rhyme with *bore*. Some Army people pronounce the word—apropos of the Royal Tournament—as [tur-nə-mənt], first syllable to rhyme with *burr*. Other Army people consider this pronunciation 'frightfully Oxford'.

TOWCESTER, Northamptonshire: [tohs-tə], the same as *toaster*.

TOWNSHEND, surname: [tounz-end], the same as *Townsend*.

TRAFALGAR: [trə-fal-gə], accent on the second syllable. But this is not the way the Spaniards pronounce this Spanish name. As is indeed pointed out by G. K. Chesterton:
'The day of Trafalgar is Spanish in name
And the Spaniards refuse to pronounce it the same'
—*Songs of Education: II Geography* vv. 31–2.
Newbolt uses the Spanish accentuation:
'When Nelson sailed for Trafalgar
With all his country's best,
He held them dear as brothers are,
But one beyond the rest'
—*Northumberland*, stanza 2.

TRAIT: [tray], no final T, to rhyme with *bay*. NOT [trayt], with final T, rhyming with *bait*.

TRAJECTORY: [traj-ek-tri], accent on first syllable. OR [trə-jekt-ə-ri], accent on second.

TRANSITIVE: [trahns-it-iv], first syllable to rhyme with *France*. NOT [tranz-it-iv], first syllable rhyming with *cans*.

TRANSLATE: [trahns-layt], first syllable to rhyme with *France*. NOT [trans-layt], first syllable rhyming with *manse*.

167

TRANSMISSION: [tranz-mish-ən], first syllable to rhyme with *bans*. NOT [trahnz-mish-ən], first syllable to rhyme with *barns*.

TRANSPARENT: [trans-pεə-rənt], first syllable to rhyme with *manse*; or [trahns-pεə-rənt], first syllable to rhyme with *France*. NOT [trans-pah-rənt]; or [trahns-pa-rənt], last part to rhyme with *arrant*.

TRANSPORT, noun: [trans-pawt], first syllable to rhyme with *manse*. OR [trahns-pawt], first syllable to rhyme with *France*. Verb: the same, but accent on second syllable.

TRANSVAAL: [trahnz-vahl], first syllable to rhyme with *barns*. NOT [tranz-vahl], first syllable rhyming with *bans*.

TRAPES, also spelt TRAIPSE: [tray-pəs], to rhyme with *shape us*. OR [trayps], to rhyme with *shapes*.

TRAVERSE: [trav-urs], accent on first syllable. NOT [trə-vurs], accent on second.

TRIESTE: [tree-yest], two syllables. OR [tree-yest-i], three.

TROPHY: [trohf-i], first syllable to rhyme with *oaf*. [trof-i], first syllable to rhyme with *doff*, is now not much used.

TROUGH: [trawf], to rhyme with *wharf*; or [trof], to rhyme with *doff*. NOT [trʌf], rhyming with *stuff*.

TROWBRIDGE, Wiltshire: [troh-brij], first syllable to rhyme with *hoe*. NOT [trou-brij], first syllable rhyming with *how*.

TRYST: [trist], to rhyme with *wrist*. OR [treist], to rhyme with *priced*. But the word is a literary one, hardly known in normal speech.

168

TUCSON, U.S.A.: [tʊ-sawn], accent on second syllable, which rhymes with *born*. No C.

TURQUOISE: [tur-kwahz], second syllable to rhyme with *bars*. NOT [tur-kwoiz], second syllable rhyming with *boys*.

Madame TUSSAUD'S: [tə-sohz], no D, second syllable to rhyme with *blows*. NOT [tə-sawdz], with D, second syllable the same as *swords*.

TWADDELL, surname: [twod-el]. The accent is on the second syllable, doubtless because, if it were on the first, the name would be the same as the word *twaddle*.

TWOHOMEY, Irish surname: [toom-i], to rhyme with *gloomy*.

TYRANNICAL: [tɛi-ran-ik-əl]. OR [ti-ran-ik-əl].

TYROL: [tir-əl], to rhyme with *Cyril*. OR [tir-ol], second syllable to rhyme with *doll*. OR [tir-ohl], second syllable to rhyme with *dole*—accent on second syllable.

TYRWHITT, surname: [tir-it], to rhyme with *spirit*.

UIST, Hebrides: [yoost], to rhyme with *roost*. NOT [yoo-wist], two syllables.

UNPRECEDENTED: [ʌn-pres-ə-dent-id], second syllable to rhyme with *less*. NOT [ʌn-prees-ə-dent-id], second syllable rhyming with *lease*.

UNTOWARD: [ʌn-toh-wəd], three syllables, second the same as *toe*. NOT [ʌn-twawd], two syllables.

URQUHART, Scotch surname: [urk-ət].

169

URUGUAY: [yaw-rə-gwạy], last syllable to rhyme with *bay*. OR [yaw-rə-gwẹi], last syllable to rhyme with *buy*.

USHANT, France: [ʌsh-ənt].

UTAH: [yọọ-tə], to rhyme with *pewter*. But the American pronunciation is [yọọ-taw], second syllable the same as *tore*.

UTRECHT: [yoo-trẹkt], accent on second syllable. OR [yọọ-trekt], accent on first.

UTTOXETER, Staffordshire. The older pronunciations are [ʌks-i-tə], first syllable to rhyme with *sucks*, and [ʌch-i-tə], first syllable to rhyme with *such*, accent on first syllable. But, to-day, most people say [yʊ-tọks-i-tə], accent on second syllable, which rhymes with *box*.

VALET: [vạl-et], to rhyme with *mallet*. NOT [vạl-ay], rhyming with *ballet*.

VANBURGH, surname: [vạn-brə], second syllable the same as last syllable of *Edinburgh*.

VARIEGATED: [vẹə-rig-ayt-id], second syllable the same as *rig*. The pronunciation [vẹə-ryə-gayt-id], first part to rhyme with *area*, is also possible.

VASE: [vahz], to rhyme with *bars*. NOT [vayz], rhyming with *pays*; or [vawz], rhyming with *paws*.

VAUGHAN, Welsh surname: [vawn], to rhyme with *dawn*.

VAULT: [vawlt]. NOT [volt].

170

VAUX, surname. Usually [vawks], to rhyme with *forks*. But sometimes [voh], to rhyme with *foe*. Not often [voks], to rhyme with *fox*.

VAUXHALL, London: [voks-hawl], the two syllables being equally stressed. But the car is [voks-hawl], accent on the first syllable only.

VAVASOUR, surname: [vav-ə-sə], accent on first syllable, which rhymes with *have*.

VEHEMENT: [vee-yə-mənt], no H. NOT [vee-hə-mənt], with H.

VENABLES, surname: [ven-ə-bəlz], accent on first syllable.

VENEZUELA: [ven-ə-zwayl-ə], third syllable to rhyme with *pail*. OR [ven-ə-zweel-ə], third syllable to rhyme with *peel*.

VENISON: [ven-zən], two syllables. NOT [ven-i-zən], three.

VENUE: [ven-yʋ], to rhyme with *menu*. But a frenchified pronunciation is often heard.

Cape VERDE *Islands*: [vurd], to rhyme with *bird*.

VERMOUTH: [vεə-mʋt], first syllable to rhyme with *bear*, second with *foot*. The pronunciation [vur-mooth], first syllable to rhyme with *fur*, second with *tooth*, is now virtually obsolete. Accent on first syllable.

VERSION: [vursh-ən]. But [vurzh-ən] is sometimes heard.

VERTIGO: [vur-tee-goh], accent on second syllable. OR [vur-ti-goh], accent on first.

VERULAM, peer's title: [ver-ʋ-ləm]. NOT [ver-yʋ-ləm], second syllable the same as that of *nephew*.

171

VERVE: [vurv], to rhyme with *nerve*. OR [vɛəv], to rhyme with *there 've* (i.e. *there have*).

VEZEY, surname: [ve̞e̞-zi], to rhyme with *easy*. NOT [ve̞z-i], first syllable rhyming with *fez*.

VIA: [vah], to rhyme with *car*. OR [vɛiə], to rhyme with *higher*. NOT [veeə], the same as *veer*.

VICE VERSA: [ve̞is-i-vu̞rs-ə], four syllables, first part to rhyme with *dicy*. NOT [ve̞is-vu̞rs-ə], three syllables, first rhyming with *dice*.

VICTUALLERS: [vi̞t-ləz], to rhyme with *Hitler's*. NOT [vi̞k-tə-ləz], three syllables, with C.

VIENNA: [vi-ye̞n-ə], accent on second syllable; [ve̞e̞-yen-ə], accent on first syllable, is old-fashioned U.

VIETNAM: [vyet-na̱m], second syllable to rhyme with *ham*. OR [vyet-na̱ẖm], second syllable to rhyme with *harm*. Americans prefer the latter.

VIKING: [vɛi̞k-ing], to rhyme with *liking*. NOT [vi̞k-ing], rhyming with *licking*.

VIOLA, musical instrument: [ve̞e̞-yə-lə], accent on first syllable; or [vi-yo̱ẖ-lə], accent on second. NOT [vɛi-yo̱ẖl-ə], first syllable the same as *vie* and accent on second.

VITAMIN: [vi̞t-ə-min], first syllable to rhyme with *bit*. OR [ve̞it-ə-min], first syllable to rhyme with *bite*.

VITUPERATE: [vit-yo̱o̱-pə-rayt], first syllable to rhyme with *bit*. OR [vɛit-yo̱o̱-pə-rayt], first syllable to rhyme with *bite*.

172

VLADIVOSTOK: [vlad-i-vọs-tok], accent on third syllable. OR [vlad-i-vos-tọk], accent on last.

VOLT: [vohlt], to rhyme with *jolt*. The pronunciation [volt] is now not much used.

VOODOO: [vọọ-doo], accent on first syllable. NOT [vʊ-dọọ], accent on second.

W: [dʌb-əl-yoo], with the L of *double*. NOT [dʌb-i-yoo], without it.

WADDELL, surname: [wod-ẹl], accent on second syllable.

WAFT: [wahft]. OR [wawft], to rhyme with *dwarfed*.

WAINSCOT: [wẹn-skət], first syllable to rhyme with *pen*. NOT [wa̱yn-skət], first syllable rhyming with *pain*.

WAISTCOAT: [wẹs-kət], first syllable to rhyme with *less*, no T. NOT [wa̱yst-koht], first syllable the same as *waste*, with T.

WALDEGRAVE, peer's title: [wa̱wl-grayv], two syllables, no D, first syllable to rhyme with *crawl*.

WALMESLEY, surname: [wa̱wmz-li], first syllable the same as *warms*.

WALRUS: [wa̱wl-rəs], first syllable to rhyme with *crawl*. NOT [wọl-rəs], first syllable rhyming with *doll*.

WALTHAM *Abbey*: [wa̱wl-təm]. NOT [wa̱wl-thəm].

WAUCHOPE, Scotch surname: [wọk-ʌp], first syllable to rhyme with *lock* (but with Scotch *ch* in *loch* for [k]), second syllable

173

the same as *up*. In England the name is often pronounced [wa̱w̱k-ʌp], the same as *walk-up*, or [wa̱w̱-hohp], second syllable the same as *hope*. But NOT [wa̱w̱-chohp], with CH.

WAUGH, surname: [waw], the same as *war*.

WEDNESBURY, Staffordshire: [we̱nz-bər-i], three syllables, no D.

WEDNESDAY: [we̱nz-di], two syllables, no D. NOT [we̱d-ənz-day], three syllables, first part to rhyme with *deadens*.

WELCHMAN, surname: [we̱lsh-mən], the same as *Welshman*.

WELLESLEY, surname: [we̱lz-li], first syllable the same as *wells*.

WELWYN, Hertfordshire: [we̱l-in], to rhyme with *Helen*.

WEMYSS, Scotch surname: [weemz], to rhyme with *dreams*.

WERE: [wɛər], to rhyme with *bear*. OR [wur], to rhyme with *burr*. OR, in some sentences in which it is not fully stressed, [wə].

WESLEYAN: [we̱z-li-yən], first syllable to rhyme with *fez*. OR [we̱s-li-yən], first syllable to rhyme with *less*.

West BROMWICH, Staffordshire: [bro̱m-ij], first syllable to rhyme with *Tom*. NOT [brʌm-ij], first syllable rhyming with *rum*.

WESTMINSTER: [we̱s-mins-tə], accent on first syllable, no first T. NOT [we̱st-mi̱ns-tə], the first two syllables being equally stressed.

Weston super MARE: [mɛə], the same as *mare*. NOT [ma̱-ri], the same as *marry*, which would be pedantic.

WHATMOUGH, surname: [wǫt-moh], second syllable the same as *mow*.

WHEWELL, surname: [hool], to rhyme with *fool*. OR [hyǫǫ-wəl], to rhyme with many people's pronunciation of *jewel*.

WHILOM: [wɛil-əm], to rhyme with *pile 'em* (i.e. *pile them*). NOT [wil-ǫhm], accent on second syllable.

WIDECOMBE, Devon: [wid-i-kəm], three syllables.

WILDEBEEST: [wɛil-di-beest]. OR the Afrikaans pronunciation.

WILLOUGHBY, surname: [wil-o-bi].

Willoughby de BROKE, peer's title: [brʊk], the same as *brook*.

WIND, noun: [wind], to rhyme with *sinned*. But, in poetry, often [wɛind], to rhyme with *signed*.

WINSTANLEY, surname: [win-stan-li], accent on second syllable.

WISBECH, Cambridgeshire: [wiz-beech], second syllable the same as *beach*. NOT [wiz-bek], second syllable the same as *beck*.

WOBURN, Bedfordshire: [wǫǫ-bən], first syllable the same as *woo*. But most people say [wǫh-bən], first syllable the same as *woe*.

WODEHOUSE, surname: [wud-hous], first syllable the same as *wood*. NOT [wǫhd-hous], first syllable the same as *woad*.

WOLLASTON, surname: [wʊl-əs-tən], accent on first syllable, which is the same as *wool*. NOT [wǫl-əs-tən], first syllable rhyming with *doll*; or [wʊl-as-tən], or [wol-as-tən], accent on second syllable.

175

WOLSEY, surname: [wu̯l-zi], first syllable the same as *wool*.

WOLSTENHOLME, surname: [wu̯l-stən-hohm], first syllable the same as *wool*. NOT usually [wol-stən-hohm], first syllable rhyming with *doll*.

WOODROFFE, surname: [wu̯d-rʌf], second syllable the same as *rough*.

WOOLWICH, London: [wu̯l-ij], second syllable to rhyme with *ridge*. No second W. NOT [wu̯l-ich], second syllable rhyming with *rich*.

WYCOMBE, Buckinghamshire: [wik̯-əm], to rhyme with *pick 'em* (i.e. *pick them*).

WYKEHAM, surname: same as preceding.

WYMONDHAM, Norfolk: [wi̯nd-əm], the same as *Wyndham*. NOT [wɛi̯-mənd-həm], as spelt.

YEAR: [yeeə], to rhyme with *hear*. NOT [yur], rhyming with *her*.

YEAST: [yeest], to rhyme with *beast*. NOT [yest], rhyming with *best*, which is a North Country pronunciation.

YESTERDAY: [yest̯-ə-di], with just one accent—on the first syllable. NOT [yest-ə-da̯y], the first and third syllables being equally stressed.

YONGE, surname: [yʌng], the same as *young*.

YOUNGHUSBAND, surname: [yʌng-hʌz-bənd], accent on second syllable.

YPRES, Belgium. Pronounced in the French way. The soldiers' pronunciation of the 1914–18 War was [wɛi̯-pəz], the same as *wipers*.

YUGOSLAVIA: [yoo-goh-slaẖv-yə], third syllable to rhyme with *halve*. NOT [yoo-goh-slạyv-yə], third syllable the same as *slave*.

ZEBRA: [zẹẹb-rə], first syllable to rhyme with *glebe*. NOT [zẹb-rə], first syllable rhyming with *deb*.

ZEEBRUGGE, Belgium. Known from the 1914–18 War: [zi-brʌg-ə], last part to rhyme with *Rugger*.

ZOOLOGICAL. The 'correct' pronunciation is [zoh-ə-lọj-i-kəl], five syllables, first to rhyme with *toe*, and this pronunciation is the one in technical use. [zoo-lọj-i-kəl], four syllables, first to rhyme with *too*, is much heard, as is also the mixture of the two, [zoo-wə-lọj-i-kəl]. Hence the abbreviation *Zoo* = *Zoological Gardens*.

ZUIDER ZEE: [zɛi-də-zẹẹ], accent on last syllable, which rhymes with *tea*. This is not the Dutch pronunciation.